The Tao *of* Forgiveness

JEREMY P. TARCHER/PENGUIN

a member of Penguin Group (USA) Inc.

New York

The Tao *of* Forgiveness

The Healing Power of Forgiving Others and Yourself

WILLIAM MARTIN

JEREMY P. TARCHER/PENGUIN
Published by the Penguin Group
Penguin Group (USA) Inc., 375 Hudson Street, New York, New York 10014, USA • Penguin Group (Canada),
90 Eglinton Avenue East, Suite 700, Toronto, Ontario M4P 2Y3, Canada (a division of Pearson Penguin
Canada Inc.) • Penguin Books Ltd, 80 Strand, London WC2R 0RL, England • Penguin Ireland,
25 St Stephen's Green, Dublin 2, Ireland (a division of Penguin Books Ltd) • Penguin Group (Australia),
250 Camberwell Road, Camberwell, Victoria 3124, Australia (a division of Pearson Australia Group Pty Ltd) •
Penguin Books India Pvt Ltd, 11 Community Centre, Panchsheel Park, New Delhi–110 017, India •
Penguin Group (NZ), 67 Apollo Drive, Rosedale, North Shore 0632, New Zealand (a division
of Pearson New Zealand Ltd) • Penguin Books (South Africa) (Pty) Ltd, 24 Sturdee Avenue,
Rosebank, Johannesburg 2196, South Africa

Penguin Books Ltd, Registered Offices: 80 Strand, London WC2R 0RL, England

Most Tarcher/Penguin books are available at special quantity discounts for bulk purchase for sales promotions,
premiums, fund-raising, and educational needs. Special books or book excerpts also can be created to fit specific
needs. For details, write Penguin Group (USA) Inc. Special Markets, 375 Hudson Street, New York, NY 10014.

Library of Congress Cataloging-in-Publication Data

Martin, William, date.
The tao of forgiveness : the healing power of forgiving others and yourself / William Martin.
p.   cm.
ISBN 978-1-58542-789-5
1. Forgiveness—Religious aspects—Taoism.   2. Taoism.   3. Laozi. Dao de jing.   I. Title.
BL1900.L36M325   2010   2010000611
299.5'14432—dc22

Printed in the United States of America
1   3   5   7   9   10   8   6   4   2

BOOK DESIGN BY NICOLE LAROCHE

For Nancy, as always.
She sees me with her Tao Mind
and points me to my own.

Contents

Preface

My love affair with the classic wisdom poetry contained in Lao-tzu's *Tao Te Ching* is entering its fifth decade. My understanding of his words has shifted and settled into new niches in my mind with each change in circumstance and life situation. It guided me in my twenties to remain entranced with the Mystery of the Tao when my conditioning wanted everything, including spirituality, to be certain and clear. It comforted me in my thirties and early forties as the joys and trials of parenting put an end to many dearly held illusions. It danced and romped with me as my forties and fifties brought me more love and joy than I could have dreamed possible. It beckoned me to take the hesitant step over the hump of fifty-five and into the world of AARP, senior discounts, and mortality. I've tried to give some account of these stages in my life through my earlier books: *The Parent's Tao Te Ching, The Couple's Tao Te Ching,* and *The Sage's Tao Te Ching.*

Some experts on the craft of writing advise, "Write what you know." I have spent my career writing about all the things I *don't know.* I wrote a book on parenting when the only thing I knew was every possible mistake a parent can make. I wrote about love between two people—a mystery that no one could possibly really know anything about. And I wrote about growing old with grace and courage. I'll let you know how that turns out.

I am grateful to the wisdom of Lao-tzu, whose classic line in chapter 56 of the *Tao Te Ching* is often translated: "Those who know, don't speak. Those who speak, don't know." Those words seem to be an admonition to keep one's mouth shut and not prattle on with a façade of wisdom. Then again, perhaps they are a mere caution that, whenever someone speaks or writes, they have taken the risk of speaking the unutterable and writing the unfathomable, and their words are to be taken with caution.

Now, in my early sixties, I have been given the opportunity to look at Lao-tzu once again, this time from the perspective of *Forgiveness.* So I pick up again the burden of one who does not know, but who speaks anyway, because I am beginning to experience a glimpse that forgiveness is the very stuff that holds the whole cosmos together. That it is not just a nice, moral, good-person thing to do, but is part of the very nature of the Tao Itself. I am discovering that for-giveness, like the Tao, is the very water in which we human fish swim and live and breathe. It's been a wondrous and freeing discovery.

BILL MARTIN
Chico, California
January 2009

Introduction

The Practice of Forgiveness

Every expectation that is not met, every disappointment, every shameful memory, every regret for things done or undone—great or small—forms the content for the processes of clinging or aversion, grasping or pushing away. Over the years this process narrows and restricts our experience of life, making it seem far less than the wondrous adventure it truly can be.

The Tao of Forgiveness is a practice of laying down that process, letting go of all that has happened, keeping only the openhearted wisdom that has bloomed from the soil of our triumphs, our disappointments, and our mistakes. It is a path of freedom and spacious acceptance. It is the grace-filled life for which we all long, and which we have forgotten has been ours all along.

The Tao

If you are not familiar with Lao-tzu's wonderful wisdom, may I invite you to obtain a copy of his *Tao Te Ching* and use it as a companion to this book on the journey of forgiveness. It is available in dozens of translations, including my own (*A Path and a Practice,* Da Capo Press). It is a small book, only eighty-one short verses of wisdom poetry, written more than 2,500 years ago. Yet it remains one of the most translated and venerated books of both Eastern and Western cultures. It sets out the basic themes of the Tao that I will be using as a foundation for this book on the practice of forgiveness.

In *The Tao of Forgiveness,* the important word is *Tao.* Directly seeking forgiveness itself will leave us stuck in a maze of impossible contradictions. If we find the Tao in any situation, however, we will find forgiveness to be a natural consequence. So this book presents a practice that will help us discover the Tao waiting within our own minds and hearts. Finding that, we will find the forgiveness we seek.

Tao (pronounced Dao) can be translated in many ways, from a simple "path up to the front door," to the sublime "The Way the Cosmos Unfolds Itself." It is the Mystery behind all mysteries, the God behind all gods, the Unnameable behind all names. We can speak about it, but as Lao-tzu taught, the words we use are mere imperfect pointers and are not the Tao Itself.

Like the Tao, forgiveness cannot be presented in a linear fashion. It cannot be discovered through a series of premises presented in a logical progression, culminating in the "Aha, now I have got it!" experience we Western people so enjoy. I wish it were different. It would be more gratifying, and probably more popular, to write a book on forgiveness that promised a grasp of and control over the subject—*Ten Tidy Tips to Total Forgiveness.*

That is not possible. I am constrained by the nature of the Tao Itself to offer stories, parables, poetry, and meditative exercises. There is no way to predict what you will experience as you read the stories and work with the suggestions. If you are like me, it will depend on the mood you are in when you read. Sometimes, when I read a book, there will be a spacious gap in my mind that allows something entirely new, spurred by the words I read but not contained by them, to arise in my experience. At other times, my reading is merely a search for pre-packaged ideas that fit my familiar forms of thought, comforting me in my conditioned notions of what life is and who I am. It has been my experience that the combination of story, poetry, and suggestion can be effective in searching out those mind-gaps that help open us to the Tao. It is my hope that my words will provide that for you—a doorway into an experience of your own Tao Nature.

Two Minds

Forgiveness is not confined by any particular religious belief system. It is, at its heart, a direct experience of the spacious unconditional acceptance found in the Tao and made available to us through what I call our Tao Mind. This Tao Mind is active whenever we are immersed in the non-interpretive, wide-open wonder and awe of just "what is" in the present moment. It is the Tao Mind that watches a flock of Canada geese play hide-and-seek with scudding clouds without adding layers of labels and interpretations such as "Canada geese, windy day, getting to be winter, got to get the firewood chopped, wonder where they're going to spend the winter." The Tao Mind just experiences the wonder of cloud-cold-wind-geese with an "Ahhh." It is the same with forgiveness. There is a moment when thoughts and concepts such as "letting go, making restitution, she shouldn't have said that, why did I do that?" give way to the "Ahhh" of freedom.

This direct experience is juxtaposed with a more conditioned experience of thought and concept. Our brains, especially the left hemispheres, are designed to take the vast amount of input impinging on our senses in every moment and sort, categorize, remember, and form conceptual frameworks—connections of categories—from that input. By the time we are three or four years old the brain has formed, in addition to all the other conceptual frameworks, a concept called "Me."

This conditioned mind that we each have learned to call "me" is very difficult to bring under scrutiny. It is like attempting to use the eye to look at the eye. The best we can do is to investigate the reflections—the ways in which this thing we call "ego," or conditioned mind, manifests itself; the ways in which it behaves and interacts with life. This investigation is one of the primary tasks of the practice of a Tao of Forgiveness, for it is the conditioned mind, or ego in its many forms, that does the resenting, clinging, shaming, blaming, wanting, needing, judging, and suffering that limit our experience of the intrinsic forgiveness of the Tao Nature and of our Tao Mind.

The Masks We Wear

One helpful tool in this investigation is the concept of the "persona"—from the Greek word meaning "mask." It is the root of the generalized term "personality," which is actually a plural noun encompassing the whole cast of personas that make up the ego identity. In this book I will use the word "sub-personality" to indicate a specific persona with identifiable characteristics, needs, wants, reactions, and behaviors. It is the sub-personality that causes the somewhat eerie experience of feeling "not myself today," or the confusion of enjoying something one day and being irritated and impatient with the same thing the next day. We are a combination of many "selves," each with opinions and needs that make the process of forgiveness a complex practice.

This conditioned mind with all of its sub-personalities is not a bad thing. Both the Tao Mind and the conditioned mind are part of the fullness of our humanity. It is a marvel that we are able to shift from the direct experience of the Tao Mind to the interpretation of that experience in the conditioned mind, and back again to the Tao Mind. It is important, however, to remember that the essence of forgiveness itself is available only to the direct experience of the Tao Mind. It is that direct unconditional experience to which I am pointing with the conditional words of this book.

The Stories

I have written twenty-three short stories that I hope will open small windows in our struggles for forgiveness. The Tao has always been communicated through story. It is not the lengthy discourses of teachers that find root in human consciousness. It is the stories. I have written some of these stories based on classic tales from Taoist and Buddhist teachers. Others I have spun out of the threads of my own experience. Let them amuse, instruct, inspire, confuse, or frustrate you in any way they will. Notice as you read that your experience will not necessarily be smooth and easy. Life is not smooth and easy. It contains every emotion and sensation possible. Pay attention to your own experience and to the subtle stirrings of the freedom of forgiveness in your Tao Mind. Pay attention also to the voices from your conditioned mind that continually add commentary designed to keep you believing what you have always believed and experiencing what you have always experienced.

The Use of Questions, Guided Experience, and Poetry

Following each story in this book I have included sections titled "Questions for Your Tao Mind," "A Tao Mind Exercise," and "A Tao Mind Meditation." The questions are open-ended and designed to give you a way of reflecting on how the practice of forgiveness might be operating, or be stymied, in your life. There are no "right" answers to these questions. Think about them. Meditate on them. Use them if they are helpful.

The exercises are suggested activities that may help you take the intuitive step into the freedom and release of forgiveness. Sometimes taking a walk, meditating on a certain memory, or even smashing plates against a back fence may be the simple step that breaks loose the hold conditioned mind has on our perspective. In that moment, the Tao Mind is waiting and the Tao of Forgiveness rushes through us like a cleansing stream.

If you are like me, you may tend to skip over the exercises. ("I don't do exercises.") Part of my conditioning is invested in a process called "Let's get to the meat." This process is actually more accurately called "Stay in your head. The heart is too vulnerable." I would encourage you to look at your own experience here. It often takes something that seems silly and contrary to our usual way of doing things to open our intuition. If you are trying to get a grip on forgiveness with your conditioned mind, please consider these little invitations to try another way.

The "Tao Mind Meditations" are verses written in the style of Taoist wisdom literature—short thoughts that, like the exercises, are designed to help the intuitive leap. Perhaps you can use them as tools in silent meditation. If you like, you can rewrite them to fit you own practice of the moment. Perhaps one will even irritate you and cause you to think, "What in the world? Nuts to this!" Wonderful. Irritation can sometimes open up the kind of space we need.

I have attempted to be coherent and clear, but there is no linear path through this book. You may enjoy skipping from story to story, or you may benefit from reading the book straight through to give you an immersion in the Tao of Forgiveness that cannot be captured piecemeal. I hope that the book will remain on your shelf or end table for a long time. It is my experience that stories can be revisited after the space of several months or even years and, because a different "person" is reading, a deeper intuitive understanding arises. One or two stories may cause an "Aha!" experience on their first reading. Others may engender a "What?" experience today and an "Oh, I see!" experience next month. Who knows? This is the Tao working, and if I try to predict, tame, and categorize *that*, we are both in trouble.

Self/Other

I assumed that I would separate the stories and exercises in this book into two sections—one that dealt primarily with forgiving ourselves, the other that focused on the forgiveness of others outside ourselves. I couldn't do it. The more I explored the mysterious workings of forgiveness in the Tao Mind, the more I found what I should have realized right from the start—that there is no separation between self and other.

Here at The Still Point Center in Chico, California, where I teach, we have a recitation that we say together at the beginning of each morning meditation period. It expresses many elements of our practice together and closes with the words "There is no self and other, as the awareness of pure, undisturbed consciousness slips into all consciousness."

At the level of conditioned mind, there certainly is a "self" and an "other." This is a perspective of reality that is not wrong, just inadequate. From the perspective of the Tao Mind, the phrase "There is no self and other" is a truth that guides our experience of forgiveness. The "Golden Rule," expressed in many traditions, is actually not a proscriptive "rule" of the way we should behave but, in fact, a "law"—a statement of the way we *do* behave. We *do* treat others the way we treat ourselves and we *do* treat ourselves the way we treat others. Forgiveness is one process—a way of letting go of our conditioned clinging and resisting, whether it be applied to our guilt and shame toward ourselves or to our disappointment and resentment toward others. It sometimes seems as if we forgive ourselves more easily than we forgive others. At other times we wail, "I forgive others but I just can't seem to forgive myself." But even though forgiveness may be seen to have two sides, self and other, it is only one coin.

On occasion we will look outward at others and feel a sense of letting go, of actually seeing that we no longer carry resentment or anger toward them, we *have* forgiven them. But when we switch our attention back to ourselves, we enter a different process. We tighten our grip and once again cling with passionate resolve to guilt and shame. The two processes can, of course, be reversed—clinging to the faults of others and releasing our own. As we continue to practice we will find that the Tao Mind is the place of freedom for both self and other.

The practice of forgiveness is the practice of releasing—whether it be internal shame or externally projected anger and resentment. Some of the stories in this book focus on self-forgiveness, some on the forgiveness of others. I have attempted to present them in such a manner as to enable the exploration of the process of letting go, because it is always an inner work. It is we who are clinging—either to shame or to resentment. It is we who are looking for release and freedom. There is no self and other. Forgiveness is about our own life, our own movement from conditioned mind as the only source of self-identity to the "pure, undisturbed consciousness" that is our Tao Mind.

Dear friend, the truth is that we are all clinging to resentments, disappointments, and secret or not-so-secret shames that limit and seek to determine our experience of life. But the deeper truth is that, in the ever-flowing river of the

Tao, letting go is possible and a life of freedom, tempered by the tenderness of an open heart, is waiting for us. If this book does not help your journey into this freedom, I ask you to "forgive me." If just one story in this little book opens your life to the reality of spacious grace—well, as the Taoist Master said when asked the secret of life—"Wow!"

Already There

There is nowhere to go for forgiveness.

For many years John would come and stand in front of the gate marked "This Way to Forgiveness." It was a large wrought-iron gate in an electrified fence. Both gate and fence were marked with large ominous signs that warned, "Danger—High Voltage!"

But John kept coming back. He could see through the gate into a paradise of green forests, cascading streams, and fertile fields. The sight of such nurture and luxury just out of reach made life on his side of the gate more and more miserable. He looked around at the wilderness on his side and felt a deep despair at the parched, barren landscape. He longed to get across the fence, through the gate, somehow to gain entrance to the paradise beyond.

Finally one day he realized that he would rather be dead than continue to live with such torment. Taking a deep breath, he reached out and pushed against the electrified bars of the gate. It swung open easily, no shock, no searing current charring his body. He stood transfixed for a moment, then slowly walked through the open gate into the welcoming fields.

The warm sun fell on his face and the gentle breeze soothed the warmth just enough. Delicious smells drifted into his nose and his eyes took in a land even more beautiful than what he had seen through the bars. Sighing in relief, he turned to look back at the wilderness from which he had escaped and saw nothing but the same beautiful countryside as far as the eye could see—no fence, no gate, no wilderness.

The human brain is a marvelous organ, capable of sorting, categorizing, storing, and making connections between the categories it has created. It is also capable of more mysterious functions such as creating, imagining, wondering, and feeling.

Through its functions of sorting, categorizing, and storing it forms what can be called conditioned mind. As a child matures, the constant categorization work of the brain forms the awareness of an "I" as a separate category within the brain. This "I" is often referred to as the Ego, or center of self-identity. This Ego is a conditioned mind, in that it is formed by the conditions in which the person lives—the family, community, society, geography, climate, flora, fauna, assumptions, difficulties, physical makeup, diet—all of the almost infinite elements that impinge upon the senses of the person from moment to moment.

This conditioned mind is a wonderful construct. It enables me to have an individual human experience of the mysterious Tao Life. It creates a fascinating sense of "me"—a me that is different from every other "me" in the Universe. This "me" has a unique perspective of reality, based on the conditions of my life and the way they have been interpreted and stored by my particular brain.

Yet for all its benefits, this conditioned mind creates a sense of separation from all other beings, from the world, from life, and from the Tao Itself. It has built the fence and the gate that keeps itself from freedom and joy for which it longs. This sense of being shut out is an illusion for it exists only in the synapses of the brain. It is, however, a very *real* illusion. Most people spend the greatest part their life believing this illusion and suffering very real consequences of fear, disappointment, resentment, and guilt based on this belief.

Good news. The very brain that has participated in creating the conditioned mind is also the organ that allows an experience of the Tao Mind—our unconditioned identity that knows itself in an entirely different manner from the conditioned mind. Our Tao Mind experiences the flow of creativity, wonder, acceptance, appreciation, power, compassion, and forgiveness that are the natural qualities, or virtues, of the Tao Itself.

Some researchers have come to see the right hemisphere of the brain as the primary location of this Tao Mind and the left hemisphere more identified with the conditioned mind. This is an oversimplification because both hemispheres are capable of many overlapping functions, but it is interesting to note that brain research seems to support the idea of two "minds," working together but each capable of quite a different experience of the "What Is" of life.

Both minds, of course, belong to the Tao and are essential to human life. It is important, however, to remember that the conditioned mind, for all its capabilities, is incapable of truly understanding and experiencing the wonder and freedom of forgiveness. It is capable of creating a category called "forgiveness." It is capable of making up rules and strategies in an attempt to define and understand this category. It is capable of talking about forgiveness, but it cannot experience the thing itself until it turns to the Tao Mind for assistance.

Once we step into our Tao Mind and feel, in the depth of our being, the freedom of forgiveness, our conditioned mind can have an increased understanding, awareness, and appreciation. Somewhere within the brain, perhaps in the corpus callosum between the two hemispheres, lies a mysterious willingness to shift attention from conditioned mind to Tao Mind, then to shift back again when appropriate. This ability to shift our attention, to go through the forbidding gate, is the key to a life of forgiveness, freedom, and happiness.

It requires only a tiny bit of willingness to change a life and a world. This willingness to shift attention to the Tao Mind will be essential to our practice of forgiveness. Without this shift our practice will bog down in one more attempt to fix, improve, tweak, and modify the conditioned mind until we finally become the "right" person. And, of course, "right" will always be defined as beyond our reach. If we could, through our conditioned mind, get it "right," we would have done it by now. Instead, our practice will gently guide us to explore a whole new way of seeing, experiencing, and being—a way that is available to us in each and every moment and that requires no fixing, improving, or tweaking.

This ability to shift the focus of our attention to Tao Mind is, at once, both simple and difficult. It is simple because it requires only willingness. It is difficult because our conditioned mind is deeply habituated to assume that it is "us" and that it is the only arena in which life actually exists. Many of its patterns have been in control of our life experience for so long that the shift to Tao

Mind is seen as a fairy tale, a myth, unrealistic, and dangerous. It will be important to treat ourselves with patience, gentleness, and compassion as we teach ourselves to step into the wonder and grace of the Tao of Forgiveness.

My conditioned mind would say, "The idea of 'Tao Mind' seems elusive to me. I'm not sure I believe in something so intangible."

Don't worry if you can't picture something called Tao Mind, understand it, or even believe in it. This practice is not about creating and clinging to one more set of beliefs. It is about paying attention and using every feeling, sensation, and experience to see how the mystery of the mind unfolds. Don't take my word for the existence of Tao Mind. Practice. Watch. See what your experience becomes. You can always go back to working only with the conditioned mind. We all know how to do that.

Questions for Your Tao Mind

- *Do you feel like you are standing outside the gate of forgiveness?*
- *What is that gate?*
- *What would it be like on the other side?*
- *What if you are already there?*

A Tao Mind Exercise

One basic way of noticing our ability to shift awareness is by "looking up." When we are identified with our conditioned mind we are usually "lost in thought." Whether we are sitting at a desk or walking in the park, our eyes tend to focus at a downward angle and we become only minimally aware of our surroundings. Our attention is on the stories, voices, criticisms, and fears that make up the bulk of our conditioned identity.

- *When you sense this lost feeling, this identification, a simple practice is to just stop for a moment. Take five relaxed and gentle breaths, feeling your chest expand and contract.*
- *Briefly take note of "where you've been"—what stories have been commanding your attention?*
- *Look around and find something on which to focus your attention—a ceramic coffee mug, a daddy longlegs spider on the wall, cottonwood leaves blowing gently in the breeze, or the dusty red color of the used bricks on the side of the old theater across the street. Let this simple object fill every aspect of your attention for as many seconds as possible.*

- *You will notice that your conditioned mind will begin a commentary designed to pull you back inside. Just notice this and once again fill your attention with the object. Then go back to whatever you were doing.*
- *This exercise is simple, yet you may notice how much resistance you feel to trying it. You may also notice how difficult it is to spend even five seconds with your attention somewhere other than your discursive thoughts. Don't worry or let any voice tell you that you're not doing it right. Even if it lasted only for two seconds, you have proved to yourself that there is a willing part of your identity that is capable of deciding where to place your attention. Isn't that marvelous? Our practice is the patient compassionate training of that small area of willingness. It is the doorway into forgiveness.*

A Tao Mind Meditation

Is there a gate
between myself and joy?
Am I forever outside

or am I already home?
Do I need forgiveness
or am I already forgiven?
Do I need to forgive,
or merely open my eyes?

Who Forgives?

Only the Tao Mind can forgive.

Master Dave sat across the small table from his student, Alex, at The Happy Frog Café. They were enjoying hot tea served in pottery mugs that were warm in their hands on a cold, wet coastal morning. As usual, neither had yet spoken, allowing the meeting to begin in comfortable silence.

Master Dave broke the silence with a question. "Well, Alex, who are you today?"

Expecting the usual "How are you?" or "What would you like to talk about?" Alex was unable to respond. He stumbled and stuttered for a moment.

Master Dave rose from his chair and said, "Let's meet again tomorrow," picked up his mug of tea, and walked back to the kitchen.

Alex spent the day in confusion. "I'd better come up with an answer to that question by tomorrow," he thought. The question seemed fraught with existential meaning and he pondered potential answers carefully. He searched for some response that would sound "Zen" and profound, but everything he came up with sounded silly and phony.

The next morning Alex awoke and lay in bed in his usual early-morning fog. The question "Who am I?" appeared in his consciousness. "Well," he thought, "I'm someone who is quite confused about who he is." Immediately the confusion disappeared. "I'm someone who's confused!" he said aloud. He bounded out of bed and whistled his way into the kitchen to put on a pot of hot water for tea. As he was watching the gas flame begin to caress the bottom of the teakettle he realized he was no longer someone who was confused. "I'm someone preparing tea," he thought.

The morning unfolded in an ever-shifting awareness of changing "selves." "Someone making mush, someone taking a shower, someone thinking about work in the garden, someone afraid of getting sick . . ." At times he was vaguely aware of "Someone" compassionately watching all the "someones" come and go.

Alex watched this process all morning as he went about his work. At lunchtime he sat down at a small table at The Happy Frog Café to once again chat with Master Dave. Dave arrived at the table carrying the familiar pot of tea and two mugs. He sat down, smiled, and asked, "Well, Alex, who are you today?"

Alex thought a moment and replied, "Just a moment ago I was someone enjoying the warmth of the room. Right now I am someone who is nervous about giving you a pleasing answer."

Master Dave smiled, poured the tea, handed a mug to Alex, and said, "Interesting. Let's talk about the one who is nervous. What does he need to hear?"

How would you answer the question—right at this moment, reading this particular line of this specific book, right here and right now? Who are you today?

Answers tend to fall into certain categories:

I am someone who . . .
I am a . . .
I am feeling . . .

Central to the question of forgiveness are the questions: Who is it that forgives? Who is it that receives forgiveness? and Who is it that withholds forgiveness? When we look to certain parts of our ego-structure for actions and attitudes of forgiveness, we are looking in all the wrong places and making impossible demands. When we are looking to the part of our identity that is rooted in the Tao, the whole process of forgiveness happens as naturally as breathing.

Our conditioned nature is so familiar, so deeply rooted in the synapses of our brain, that we mistakenly believe that it *is us*. When asked to say something about "who we are," we invariably describe some aspect of our conditioned nature. Few of us would reply to someone who asked us to tell them something about ourselves, "I am an expression of the ever-present yet ever-changing Tao." (We may find our conversations more interesting if we were to give it a try sometime.) Yet there is a power and energy of life that is intrinsic to our basic nature and the true source of our identity. It is our Tao Mind. It may also be called our "True Nature." It is the essential quality of our life that is always ours, even if hidden under layers of ego conditioning. It is the source of the Tao of Forgiveness.

The very nature of conditioning is that it is, well—conditional. The very nature of forgiveness is that it is unconditional. You can see the conundrum we face when we turn to the conditional and ask it for unconditional acceptance and forgiveness. It will never be able to give what is asked. Yet this is the arena in which we so often attempt to work out forgiveness.

Consider the way you begin each day. Picture that first awareness of consciousness as sleep gives way to waking life. Who is there? I don't mean what dearly beloved person may be in the bed next to us. I mean who do we wake up *as*? One way to get a clue as to our current conditioned self-identity is to listen to the stories that are being spun in the web of our thoughts. If I can get a sense of what I am being told, I have a pretty good idea of who is listening. If my mind is filled with stories about the dire possibilities of disaster looming ahead, I can be sure that a young and frightened sub-personality is the one listening.

As we practice the Tao of Forgiveness, it is helpful to pay attention to all the sub-personalities that step forward to volunteer to try to forgive or be forgiven. Each one will have his or her own feelings, opinions, and stories about the process. Each will have a desired outcome and a sense of what can or cannot be done to achieve that outcome. Some will be invested in holding on to either the guilt or the resentment. Some will just want to "feel better." Some will want to run away because facing a wounded heart feels just too terrifying. In the compassion of our Tao Mind we will find that there is room for each of these precious, frightened, and confused parts of ourselves. Each can be accepted just as they are.

Questions for Your Tao Mind

• *Is it difficult for you to think of yourself as composed of "parts"?*
• *Who are you, really?*

A Tao Mind Exercise

• *Sit in a comfortable place with your journal.*
• *Consider a current situation that stirs the basic awareness of forgiveness needs: resentment, guilt, shame, disappointment, anger, etc.*
• *Begin a list titled: "When I think of this I am one who . . ."*
• *Notice all the different feelings, sensations, thoughts, and voices that play across your mind. Jot down the aspects of "you" that these represent. You don't have to be clear or accurate. Just allow yourself a gentle sense of the various sub-personalities that might be involved in this particular process of forgiveness.*
• *Breathe deeply and imagine yourself as the spacious compassion of your Tao Mind. Ask each sub-personality, each "you," what they need from you. Imagine what your Tao Mind might say to each one.*

• *As in all of the exercises in this book, be very gentle with the "one" who is doing the exercise. You do not have to do it a certain way or experience a certain feeling. Let yourself feel and experience whatever arises. Be willing to accept both comfortable and uncomfortable feelings and thoughts without needing to adjust or change them.*

• *Conclude by standing, stretching, and breathing. Carry in your Tao Mind a compassionate awareness of all those precious personas that go into making up the mysterious "you."*

A Tao Mind Meditation

Who am I today?
I am the one reading these words.
I am the one who is hungry.
I am the one who is afraid.
I am the one who wants what he does not have.
I am the one who has what he does not want.
I am the one who loves.
I am the one who hates.

Beneath it all,
I am the One
who imagines he is all of these,
and who loves and forgives each one
with tender care.

A Sparrow Falls

Only the broken heart is an open heart.

Nine-year-old Tommy was free to roam the forests around his home and was ably coached by various adults in the practice of hunting. He occasionally accompanied his father and uncles on pheasant hunts but had never shot anything himself.

One day he was wandering a forest road near his home with his new BB gun. He spotted a sparrow in a nearby branch and immediately aimed and fired. The sparrow fell from the tree and flopped, wounded, into the tall grass. He ran over and found it huddled in the grass, its wings askew, its eyes wide, its heart beating furiously. He could tell it was suffering and the sight froze his own nine-year-old heart.

This was not food. This was suffering. He knew he had to end its misery so he shot it again. Still it lived. He had to shoot it several times at close range to end the suffering. By that time he was crying so that he could hardly see. He picked it up by a wing and carried it back to his house. His father saw him crying and asked him what had happened.

Tommy showed his father the sparrow and told him, between sobs, what he had done. His father put his hand on Tommy's shoulder and said, "It really hurts your heart, doesn't it, Tommy?" Tommy sobbed an affirmative. His father went on, "You are not a bad person. You needed to learn for yourself how harmful our actions can be. It's only by knowing this that you will develop true kindness. Do you think you will ever shoot a bird for no reason again?"

"Never!" Tommy said.

"Then this little bird died so that many others wouldn't have to. Let's bury him and thank him."

They did.

Many of us can recount stories similar to Tommy's. It may not have been a sparrow's death, but something done without awareness caused our heart to open in awareness to the harm of which we are capable—the tears of a friend or the look of sorrow on the face of a parent perhaps. We don't enjoy revisiting these memories, yet they remain lurking in the corridors of our brain, waiting for our conditioned mind to pull them out whenever it gets caught in a process of regret and shame. Suddenly here it is—that shameful scenario of childhood, young adulthood, or even just last week—being replayed in excruciating detail. Notice that it is often replayed with embellishments and emphases on certain of the most painful parts of the drama.

When we are caught like this, "drama" is exactly the right word. Our conditioning is scripting, assigning roles, and acting out a drama on the screen of our mind, often for the purpose of eliciting shame and suffering. This drama is far more than a mere memory of some event. The memory is simply the vehicle for punishment and therefore the actual event is modified to accentuate the shameful scenes and minimize any part of the incident that does not support the punishment and shame.

In contrast, our Tao Mind uses the memories of such incidents as compassionate reminders of our innate goodness. Yes, I said of our *innate goodness*. It is the goodness that resides at the center of our being that allows our heart to open in sorrow. Without this goodness we would be incapable of distinguishing which of our actions are harmful and which are helpful.

Other hunting animals do not need to make this distinction because they do no harm. They kill and eat to nourish their life and they do it without cruelty. Even the cat's seemingly cruel toying with a mouse is not perceived by the cat as cruel. It is merely the instinct of honing quick movements that is at work—a natural survival ability. Human beings are first of all animals and we instinctually take actions to care for ourselves, physically and psychologically. We pounce. We lash out. We defend. We attack. This is natural.

The wonder of the Tao Mind in humans is that it makes us capable of experiencing much more of life than just instinctual reactions. We are capable of imagining how other living beings may be feeling. We can sense the difference between harm and kindness. We have a quality within that Lao-tzu calls *Te*, or "natural virtue." This quality of *Te* dwells within all beings in a manner that is appropriate for that particular being's expression of life. For human beings, this expression manifests itself in tenderness and compassion and it reveals itself in the midst of our harmful actions.

Seeing how we do harm is the only way we learn to incorporate the virtue of compassion into our lives. Without the ability to see the harm we do, we could not cultivate compassion. Without the courage to look clearly and bravely at this harm, we bury our compassion beneath layer upon layer of fear and avoidance. Avoiding doing harm because we are afraid of disapproval is not compassion. It is fear. And rather than keep us from doing harm, this very fear provides the energy for yet more unthinking and reactive harmful actions. But our Tao Mind has no fear of looking at *anything*, because everything is used by

Tao Mind to nurture compassionate awareness. Certain memories will always bring a twinge of pain to our hearts. Tao Mind will always provide the space for this pain to move into tenderness.

If Tommy had not met an expression of Tao Mind in his father's response, what might have been the result? We can imagine that he may have found a way to cover up the pain he felt. He may have thrown the bird into the bushes, dried his tears, and pushed away the tenderness because it was too painful to feel. A tougher, harder part of him may have come into existence to protect his vulnerabilities. Birds as living beings or as honored food may have become "things"—living clay pigeons for target practice. (Even now I hear a part of my conditioning saying with an exasperated tone, "Get *over* it! It was just a sparrow, for God's sake. Grow up." Is that tone familiar to you?) Make no mistake, a life can turn on the death of a sparrow.

We all have countless vaguely remembered moments when we pushed away our natural tenderness because it felt too shameful and too vulnerable. But the young parts of us with these feelings never really go away. They hide within us and their shame creates a corresponding feeling of shame in our lives today, a shame whose content may be from our adult life but whose process is from our childhood. Why can't I let go of a moment from last month when I lashed out in anger? Because it is being fueled by a little boy still holding the broken wing of a sparrow.

It is never too late to bring the young and vulnerable parts of ourselves into the presence of our Tao Nature. As you may have guessed, Tommy in the story is me. As I write these words I feel a tender sadness for that little boy, crying as he walks along the road with a dead sparrow in his hand, wanting to talk to someone and at the same time wanting to hide.

The father in the story is not my own father. My father was a gentle and loving man but he was not there at the time of the incident. I had to figure it out in my own nine-year-old way. The father in the story is my image of the way Tao Mind would respond, indeed the way it has often responded when I have been able to take my regrets to its spacious welcome.

My conditioned mind worries: *If we accept that our harmful actions can lead to compassion, do we go ahead and do more harm so we can learn more compassion?*

I can only reply from my own experience. If I am learning compassion, why would I want to do harm? In a complex society we do learn guidelines as to the most helpful ways to express this natural compassion. If we are guided to see how unconscious actions can lead to harm, we will gradually develop skills for expressing our natural compassion. Increasing awareness of our tender and compassionate nature always leads to decreasing, rather than increasing, harm.

Questions for Your Tao Mind

- *Is a compassionate response "too soft" in certain occasions?*
- *How might a compassionate response be "sharp" or "hard" and still remain compassionate?*
- *Can tenderness and sternness be together in the same response?*

A Tao Mind Exercise

- *Do this exercise while walking—around your neighborhood, in a park, in the countryside—wherever you will have some sense of spaciousness and ease.*
- *As you walk, turn your attention to your breath. Experience the full range of your inhalation and exhalation.*
- *Imagine some small living creature that elicits a sense of tenderness in your heart—a lovely bird, a small rabbit, a friendly dog.*

- Some action of yours—anger, impulse, accident, mindlessness—has caused the death of this creature.
- Let yourself feel the sense of regret as clearly as possible.
- Let your Tao Mind take a form that will be comforting, and completely without judgment.
- Stop for a moment and place your hand over your heart. Listen carefully to what your Tao Mind may be saying. If you have trouble imagining the words, just imagine how the words might feel.
- Imagine the regret shifting ever so slightly and now being called tenderness. Notice a sense of thankfulness for the tenderness.

A Tao Mind Meditation

A sparrow falls and reveals my heart
by breaking it.
A look of pain and loss reveals my heart
by wounding it.
A compassionate touch reveals my heart
by healing it.

Anger

There is no one to blame.

A young African doctor sat in a hospital ward by the bed of a teenaged woman who was suffering from AIDS. He was curious because the woman seemed, in the past few days, to transform from an angry, depressed, and withdrawn patient into a smiling, laughing, and talkative young person. He asked her, "What has happened to you? You seem a different person than the one who first came to this hospital." She told him this story.

"When I first came here I was visited each day by a volunteer. She was a nice person, but she was very angry. She talked about the uncaring drug companies who would not supply the medicine I needed. She complained about the way the government misused money. She hated the man who gave this disease to me, even though he was my husband whom I loved.

"After a few days I began to feel that my life was one huge mistake. I felt that all I should have experienced had been taken from me. The same anger that was in her stirred in me. I began to hate my late husband. Everything in my life was wrong: the disease in my body, the choices I had made, and the actions of everyone around me. And there was no way to make it right. For a month I lived with ever-increasing anger and despair.

"One morning, a few weeks ago, a new volunteer began to visit me. There was no anger in her at all. She didn't talk much but she seemed so interested in me that I began to pour out my anger to her. As I did, all she ever said was, 'I'm so sorry, dear.' She said this in the kindest voice you can imagine.

"She never blamed anyone for what was happening. She listened to me and talked with me about my life, about my home and the animals that I loved. She laughed at my stories of my little brother and his pet rabbit. She marveled at the beauty of the countryside as we walked outside together. She did not blame me, or my husband, or anyone else. She loved me as I am—sick.

"She left a few days ago, but now I am happy. I know that my life has not been a mistake—that I am not a mistake. I would like to live longer. I probably won't, *but that is always the case for everyone, isn't it? Everyone wants to live longer. Everyone has to die. There is no one to blame. I am happy."*

I have voices within me that want to insist that blame is indeed appropriate somewhere in this story. There's something wrong here and, if something is wrong, someone must be at fault. Someone must be blamed. Who would you blame? The husband? The system? The woman? God? Is her life a mistake? A tragedy? If so, what makes it a tragedy?

These are difficult questions and have no answers that are satisfactory for our conditioned mind. The only answers possible are those that are found within the woman herself—and she found answers that helped her make sense of her life and her sickness. Perhaps it was not really answers that she found, but a perception—a spacious perception in which she and her life were viewed as they were, not as the way someone thought they should be.

The conditioned mind enjoys anger, though it would deny that it does. Anger covers up fear and energizes that part of us who wants to "kick butt and take names"—a potent feeling in the midst of situations that make us feel impotent. Conditioned mind becomes nervous when Tao Mind suggests seeing and accepting things as they are. "If we just smile and say everything is okay we are being naïve and irresponsible. If we don't get angry we'll never change anything."

But Tao Mind does not ask us to "smile," nor does it suggest that accepting things as they are is the same as saying that they are "okay." It does not even ask us not to get angry. Anger is just as acceptable to Tao Mind as any other emotion. It only asks that we practice seeing clearly how the anger diverts and dissipates our natural energy—energy that would otherwise be available for loving, compassionate, constructive action.

Here is one of the most common and widely believed lies that conditioned mind has ever proposed: that anger is necessary for change and that it leads to effective action. This feels very true, and most people believe it is true, but it is not true. The most helpful and effective change occurs as a result of the natural flow of the energy of the Tao. The Chinese word for this powerful flow is *Te. Te* has many meanings, including power, virtue, and energy. It describes a quality that is inherent in all life that, if not constricted by tension and resistance, will naturally act with compassion and effectiveness and will enable whatever change is most helpful and appropriate in any given situation.

Anger is natural, but it is not what brings change. We may find ourselves feeling angry over a particular situation, but it is not the anger that will allow us to see clearly what is truly ours to do. Our practice is to bring the anger to our Tao

Mind and see just who, among our sub-personalities, is feeling the anger and then giving this one the attention they need to ease their fear and frustration. Then and only then will the time for action arise—if it is the natural expression of our own *Te*.

How do we know when taking action is at the urging of our Tao Mind rather than our conditioned mind? I offer two guidelines for action that have greatly helped me. They were given to me by a Zen teacher who has been my wise and practical guide for many years:

If you feel the urge to involve yourself in action, go ahead with all your heart and mind, but

Don't blame anyone.

and

Don't recruit anyone.

Blame will only dissipate energy. Go ahead and explore root issues, structures, and systems if appropriate, but never with a sense of blame. If vigorous opposition to an action seems called for, do even that without blame. Blame never helps.

Recruiting others seems so natural. We feel such energy and commitment to a certain action, how can we help but recruit? Certainly an honest sharing of our enthusiasm may be contagious but that is quite different from the arm-twisting and argument that so often accompanies zeal for a project. If people are naturally attracted to what we are doing, wonderful. If they are not, let our *Te* be directed to the project itself.

Questions for Your Tao Mind

- *What situations in your life cause you to feel the most anger?*
- *Do you think your anger is necessary to bring about change?*
- *Who would you be without that feeling of anger?*
- *Why is it so hard to let go of it?*

A Tao Mind Exercise

I would never suggest that our anger is wrong. It is merely what it is—an emotion stirred by a reaction within us that someone or something is wrong and that wrongness makes us feel unsafe. Our forgiveness practice involves turning our attention, first to the one within us who is feeling that anger and fear, and then letting the natural energy of our Tao Mind, uncontaminated by this fear, direct our course.

Think of a situation that stirs all of the feelings of anger within you. (Pick up a newspaper if you are having trouble locating such a situation.)

- *What does thinking about this situation cause to happen in your body? Where do you feel your response? How would you physically soothe someone who was experiencing these sensations?*
- *What are the thoughts you have about this situation? Can you sense the possibility of stepping back just a bit from these thoughts? That is, can you imagine being the one who is having these thoughts?*
- *Is there a part of you who is afraid or anxious? The anger is often a way of standing in front of and protecting this part of you. What other things might you do to care for this frightened part?*
- *What does the frightened part want to do?*
- *What does the angry part want to do?*
- *How might the Tao Mind help:*
  - *the frightened one?*
  - *the angry one?*
  - *the situation itself?*

• • •

Now, let's try a more vigorous approach to anger. You will need: an old pillow-case, three old and chipped ceramic cups or plates (from a thrift store if you don't have any hidden in the recesses of your cupboards), and a private outdoor space in your backyard (you're going to be breaking things).

- *Stand in a relaxed position and let your mind review that which seems to be the cause of your anger. Don't try to talk yourself out of it. Feel it in its intensity.*
- *Put one of the plates or cups into the pillowcase, gather and tie the open end with a piece of twine or a rubber band, twirl it around your head several times to gather momentum, and smash it to the ground.*
- *Take a few breaths, lay the pillowcase down, and ask: "What are you feeling?" You are directing this question from your Tao Mind to the part of you feeling the anger. Listen for a response—it could be words, sensations, emotions, tears, whatever.*
- *Put another plate in the pillowcase and repeat the twirl and smash maneuver.*
- *Ask the question again. Wait for a response.*

- *Repeat the smash, question, response for a third time.*
- *You have been practicing shifting your attention from identification with your anger to identification with Tao Mind. Don't worry if you don't feel a resolution or real clarity—this is practice. (You may go through a lot of plates over a period of days or weeks.) You are looking for a practice that honors the one who is angry, yet does not let this one dictate the response or run your life.*
- *Bow to the pillowcase full of broken ceramic and empty it into the trash.*
- *Write for a bit in your journal.*

A Tao Mind Meditation

It's wrong!
It's wrong!
It's wrong!
I hate it!
I hate it!
I hate it!
(three deep breaths)
How can I help?

What do you need?
(three more breaths)
It's wrong!
I hate it!
(one deep breath)
How can I help?
What do you need?
(one deep breath)
I'm listening.
I'm here.

Benefit or Harm?

We can only do the best we know how to do.

Once, long ago in ancient China, a drought of many years' duration was bringing great misery to a small province. Year after year the people of the province waited for the rainy season to come and bring the needed nurture for the rice crop. Each year the season produced very little rain and the rice crop dwindled. Many were on the verge of starvation. Indeed, some elderly people had died of illnesses brought on by their hunger-weakened condition.

The people turned to the superstitions of their ancestors in an attempt to influence the rain. They performed rituals designed to stir whatever gods there were who might control the rain. They weren't sure these rituals would work, but they were desperate. They needed the rain.

Finally, just when the province was about to be devastated by yet another failing crop, the rainy season came with torrents. Day after day the rain poured down and the rice seedlings thrived in the flooded paddies. The crop was the biggest in memory. The people of the province once again felt the beneficent power of the Tao.

"Now," the Master asked, "do you think this was indeed a beneficent rainy season?"

"It would seem that it was," answered his student.

"So it would seem," said the Master. "The neighboring province, whose villages were situated along the banks of several rivers, experienced the worst flash floods of their history that year. The water came pouring suddenly down steep canyons and washed whole villages away, killing hundreds of men, women, and children. What do you suppose their view of that rainy season might have been?"

"That it was very harmful," said the student.

"So—benefit or harm? Can you ever know?"

I can write myself into endless circles trying to describe the complexity of the harm/benefit continuum. In the same way, the conditioned mind can tie me into knots of guilt by pointing out the harm I do no matter what course of action I choose. Are the chickens who laid these eggs living a cage-free, non-antibiotic, vegetarian life? If not, should I be buying these eggs? (Never mind the messages when I sit down to an actual chicken dinner!) And the coffee sitting by my hand here at the Naked Lounge Café—fair-trade? No. Shade-grown? No idea. Delicious? You bet. Does my next sip doom a struggling farmer in Brazil?

I remember the look on the face of a woman with whom I had a long-term intimate relationship many years ago when I told her I was leaving the relationship. How could I cause such pain, such feelings of betrayal, such grief? From that relationship I entered into love and marriage with my beloved Spouse. Benefit for me? Beyond measure. Harm for the former lover? Yes, or . . . ? She went on to have an interesting and satisfying life. Benefit? Harm? Both?

To this day, twenty years later, personalities in my head occasionally bring up that look on her face and shake their ghostly heads in disapproval. "How could you? And here you are, happy. How dare you be happy?" Well, like all of us, I did the best I knew how with what and who I was at the time. I put one foot in front of the other, causing harm and benefit willy-nilly as I went, my conditioned moral judges always quick to point out what they see as the harm done, no one really acknowledging the benefit.

The Tao Mind uses both harm and benefit as the raw materials that are used to build compassion. They are as necessary to each other as are the proton and the electron. They are part of a greater whole, of a compassionate life that cannot come into being without the interplay of the two. They seem to be opposed to each other, yet the Tao Mind is constantly using forgiveness to transform harm into empathy, openness, acceptance, compassion, and wholeness. Whether harm is intentional or unintentional, the forgiveness within the Tao Mind allows it to be integrated into the great Dance of Life in ways that bring unexpected benefit, allowing the surprises of grace to occur.

My conditioned mind argues, "Are you suggesting that a cruel, callous act is excusable just because the universe is complicated?"

No. But remember, "cruel and callous" is a label, not a fact. It may seem accurate but we might choose other ways of describing the act that would be more helpful in allowing forgiveness to facilitate appropriate reactions. Being willing to look at the act without the labels can lead us to certain helpful steps.

1. We can look with clarity and courage at the act itself with a desire to understand just what happened and what factors might have led to that act. We may find that the "cruel and callous" labels are no longer necessary.

2. With a clearer understanding we can take steps to heal the wounds that the act may have caused.

3. We can put appropriate structures in place to prevent continuing harm.

Remember, in the Tao Mind, the act is accepted as "having happened." The Tao Mind contains the forgiveness necessary so that we might be aware of the most compassionate healing act possible in the moment. No effort is wasted in judgment upon persons or actions. All energy is directed to the present-moment, naturally arising, compassionate action.

Questions for Your Tao Mind

- *Can you ever truly "harm" the Tao Mind of another person?*
- *Can another person ever truly "harm" your own Tao Mind?*
- *Are harm and benefit always relative?*
- *How does forgiveness bring harm and benefit together?*

A Tao Mind Exercise

I would suggest a two-chair approach to this mini-drama. Actually, if you are comfortable sitting on a cushion on the floor, you might use a chair and cushion setting. If you are not comfortable on the floor, put a cushion on one of the chairs. This cushion will represent your Tao Mind. Arrange both chair and cushion so they face a blank wall.

- *Sit in the chair and let your eyes relax as they look softly at the wall.*
- *Allow your mind to begin reviewing memories of incidents that stir either shame and regret, or resentment and anger.*
- *One of these memories will have a bit more "juice" than the others. Focus your attention on this one.*
- *While remaining in this chair, list all of the judgments, the regrets, the things done wrong, the harm that was done, and what these things mean about you or the other people.*
- *When you reach a stopping point and are feeling very uncomfortable, stand up and walk around for a bit, breathing deeply.*
- *Sit down on the cushion or place a cushion on the other chair and imagine yourself actually* becoming *your Tao Mind. While you are on this cushion there is nothing you need and no one to fix. Here you are experiencing the spacious perspective of the Tao.*
- *From this cushion, all of the characters in the memory are infinitely precious. With that perspective, what does your Tao Mind see?*
- *From this cushion, all of the characters in the memory are completely capable*

of whatever they are experiencing, able to deal with it creatively in their own way. With that perspective, what does your Tao Mind see?

- *From this cushion, the present moment becomes the only moment. With that perspective, what does your Tao Mind see as most compassionate for you and others—in this moment?*

- *When you feel your mind shifting to judgment and regret, get up immediately and sit in the other chair. Judgment sits here, not on the cushion. When the judgment plays itself out, stand up, stretch, and return to the cushion.*

- *Experiment with this exercise as long as you feel comfortable. End by sitting on the cushion and making a gentle bow to the wall, thanking your Tao Mind for its patient help.*

- *Watch for the tendency to judge yourself for the way the exercise unfolded. Our conditioned mind habitually takes helpful spiritual practices and turns them against us by making them one more "right/wrong" duality. You cannot do this, or any other exercise, wrong!*

A Tao Mind Meditation

I've done the best I knew to do.
I've caused harm and benefit
in known and unknown ways,
and these I lay to rest.
I offer all benefit from anything I have done
or will do,
to all beings.
I offer all harm I have done
or will do,
to my Tao Mind
to be transmuted into compassion
for the benefit of all beings.

Blessing and Curse

Expectations become limitations.

It is said that when the heavenly powers gathered at their huge conference table and considered the evolution of humans on the planet Earth, they had great concerns over the erratic behavior of these particular beings. On the one hand, the courage and occasional unselfish love that humans demonstrated clearly called a reward from heaven. On the other hand, their tendency to behave with fearful selfishness indicated that they merited heaven's punishment.

The powers debated for long hours trying to decide which course of action was most appropriate. Finally, one junior member cut through the debate and said, "Let's begin with the reward. I suggest that we bless them with a mind that is capable of remembering and imagining. That way they can learn from the past and an-

ticipate the future. Therefore they will be able to plan and create great wonders."
They all agreed that this reward was fitting so they caused it to be.

Then they turned their attention to the appropriate punishment. "How shall we
punish them?" they asked. The junior member spoke quietly with a trace of sadness.

"We already have," he said, "the blessing will also be the punishment."

There is a blessing in expectation. Counting on something or someone with reasonable certainty allows us to enjoy the pleasures of life without feeling totally
rootless. When we make an appointment with the dentist, we adopt a reasonable expectation that the office will be open and that the dentist will be available. Of course, the curse aspect of expectations is readily apparent. Sitting in a
waiting room with a toothache and a two-year-old issue of *People* magazine
brings us face-to-face with the growth of disappointment and the quick bloom-
ing of resentment. "This should not be happening."

Events in life seem to repeat themselves. The breath is drawn into the lungs
and then is exhaled out. Almost immediately this process occurs again, seemingly just like before. The conditioned mind soon creates an expectation that
this rhythm will continue, one breath after another, each pretty much the same
as before. It is not until a trauma or disease interferes with this taken-for-granted

expectation that we are startled into an awareness of the newness, the preciousness, the uniqueness of each and every breath.

The conditioned mind creates expectations with great ease. Bless its heart, it can't help doing so and we can be grateful for what is actually a very creative ability—projecting an outcome and moving toward it with some sense of direction and purpose. Like all functions of the conditioned mind, however, this ability is easily turned to unhappiness and resentment.

In the midst of a difficult series of events in my life many years ago, a friend shook his head sadly and said to me, "I expected better of you." I went home that evening with a great sense of shame and guilt. How dare I fail to meet expectations? Like most of us, I had been thoroughly trained to meet expectations. If I did, I was rewarded with approval. If I did not, disapproval could be devastating because the early formation of my identity and sense of safety depended entirely upon meeting these expectations, of myself and of the other people in my life. Yet these very expectations designed to keep me safe have turned into the prison bars of my limited conditioned life. I must turn once again to my Tao Mind, where I find the absence of expectations and the freedom to act according to my heart.

As usual, my conditioned mind protests, "If I don't expect anything from myself, I won't accomplish anything. No one would feel obligated to perform their jobs. Things would be sloppy. Tasks would be undone. Things would fall apart. People would be rudderless, without guidance."

Yet the tree does not grow because of its expectations and extraordinary self-discipline. It grows because it is its nature to do so. It is not disappointed in itself if it doesn't reach a certain height, if it is damaged by a storm, if it does not receive all the nutrients it needs, if it does not live up to some other tree's expectations. Yet it is always at work. Sometimes, in the spring, its work is very active and energetic and the growth can be seen every day. In the autumn it begins its work of withdrawal. In the winter it seems dormant but the inner healing processes are continuing. All this is done without effort, without strain, *and* without expectation.

My mind replies, "But I am not a tree. I am a human with feelings, needs, and desires—expectations."

Yes, we have both the blessing and the curse of expectations. How are we to handle that? Can we hold our expectations lightly enough that they serve as gentle guides rather than desperate and needy task-masters? One approach that I use in my practice might be helpful. I call this process "dis-identification."

When we fail to meet expectations, those of either other people or ourselves, we often experience the energy of two distinctly different kinds of sub-personalities. One type, usually formed at a very young age, quickly owns the shame and guilt. He has come to believe that his safety and well-being depend upon meeting expectations. When he senses that he has not met expectations, he expects to be punished. He thinks, "I have failed someone. There must be something wrong with me." He perceives the situation through this lens and feels in a one-down position.

A second type usually accompanies this young, guilty, shamed one. The second may feel a bit older, perhaps a teenager. The "There's something wrong with me" posture of the first sub-personality causes a reaction of anger and resentment in this older one. A rebellious, in-your-face attitude may arise in an attempt to protect us from the shameful feelings. His response is along the lines of "Don't you talk to my brother like that. Who do you think you are? We're outta here!" We feel this one's energy when we want to escape and/or lash back at any perceived criticism. Depending on circumstances and conditioning, one or the other of these will be dominant; the other will be repressed.

Familiar? These two types have become very dear to me in my life because I see them all the time. They are the most common energies around unmet expectations and disappointed plans. The process of release and forgiveness is very difficult, if not impossible, for them. Each has their identity rooted in holding on to either guilt or resentment.

In order to dis-identify, I try to imagine a more compassionate part of myself that has a perspective from which I can see these other parts of myself with more clarity and tenderness. From this dis-identified perspective, I am able to be in a dialogue with the disappointed parts of myself. Instead of the whole truth seeming to be "I am a failure," or "I am angry," I am able to see that a part of me feels like a failure, and another part of me responds with defensive anger. When I am dis-identified these are recognized as ego parts of me rather than "me."

Now I can be in a forgiving relationship with myself. I can bring compassion to my feelings of failure and blame because I am not fully identified with the one who has these feelings. In the same way, I am able to accept and understand that part of me that has feelings of anger. I don't have to fall into either guilt or resentment.

I naturally have hopes and expectations. Just as naturally, they do not turn out as imagined. Forgiveness is the process that frees my hopes and expectations to remain a blessing instead of turning into a curse. I am able to plan for the future with concentration and attention as I schedule my appointments and reach for my dreams, knowing that underneath is the spaciousness of my Tao

Mind, ready to forgive me and all others when appointments are forgotten and dreams do not quite come true.

Questions for Your Tao Mind

- *Do we have a right to expect certain things from others? From ourselves?*
- *What things fall into the category of "reasonable expectations"?*
- *What are effective responses to unmet expectations?*

A Tao Mind Exercise

It may be helpful to sit at a table with a pencil and notebook for this exercise.

- *Sit quietly and pay attention to the subtle feelings in your body for a moment.*
- *Let your memory search find a recent feeling of disappointment, of unmet expectations.*
- *See if you can find a sense of two different parts of you, each with different*

responses to the situation. One may be very dominant and the other quite hidden so watch carefully and patiently for a bit.

• Can you imagine another "part" of yourself, one closely in contact with the spaciousness of Tao Mind, relating to these two younger versions of "you" with tenderness and acceptance?

• Sit with your journal and, from the perspective of Tao Mind, ask one of these parts of you just what it is feeling. Listen carefully for a moment.

• Use your nondominant hand to write whatever comes to mind about the feelings of this young one.

• Respond from your Tao Mind with your dominant hand. Remember that Tao Mind is not interested in instructing, fixing, changing, or advising. It is only interested in listening, accepting, and expressing reassurance and tenderness.

• Ask the other part of you what it is feeling and again respond with the nondominant hand.

• If you are willing to stay with this exercise, you might ask each young part of you what it feels it needs to be safe and reassured. Is there a way that your Tao Mind can offer this reassurance?

A Tao Mind Meditation

Blessings and peace to all in me
who are disappointed.
Blessings and peace to all in me
who feel they have disappointed others.
I offer my expectations to my Tao Mind.
May they be used as gentle reminders,
released quickly when necessary,
modified gently when appropriate,
and always serve the cause of compassion.

The Sieve

Thoughts can't contain forgiveness.

"Please help me find forgiveness!" begged the woman as she knelt before the Taoist Master. *"I have longed to be free of my guilt. I have prayed, sacrificed, and studied holy writings for many years, but nothing I do makes me feel better."*

"Fill this with water," said the Master, handing her a sieve and pointing to the river. The woman looked incredulously at the sieve. *"Master,"* she whined, *"I don't . . ."*

"Go!" commanded the Master. *"Do it!"*

The woman scurried away to the riverbank and dipped the sieve into the water. The water ran out. She tried cupping one hand under the sieve, but still the water ran out. She tied her scarf around the sieve and managed to slow the water's escape, but still it ran out. Nothing she could do would keep the sieve filled with water.

She returned to the Master. "Master," she cried, "I cannot do it. No one can fill a sieve with water."

"So," the Master replied, "trying to find forgiveness with the small mind is the same. Give me the sieve."

The master took the sieve and hurled it into the river where it quickly sank to the bottom. "Now," he said, "it is filled."

The woman instantly found the forgiveness she had sought.

I love tea in the mornings. The texture of a pottery mug, the aroma of a blend of herbs wafting in the air, and the taste of the hot liquid on my tongue help me create a connection with my Tao Mind. The brewing process often brings the above story to my mind. Here at my favorite café they serve the tea in loose leaf form. The tea is placed in a small mesh container and immersed in the hot water. I would draw some interesting looks were I to attempt to pour the water into the mesh container and quickly try to drink before the liquid spilled over the table and my lap. It seems that the freedom of forgiveness is found only through the steeping process. I can't contain it in my conditioned mind. I must take the plunge into the water of the Tao Mind.

I would rather not take that plunge. I am reluctant to let go of the dry brittle leaves of my conditioned thoughts. I know that the warm flow of the Tao will soften them and enable them to release that to which they cling. That release will create nourishment and refreshment for my life, yet still I hesitate. "The water is far too hot," my conditioned mind warns. "You will be burned, maybe even drowned. Don't jump. Stay here. We'll figure it out somehow."

But we can't "figure it out." Forgiveness is not something to be figured out. I can neither receive nor give forgiveness from my conditioned mind. So why do I return again and again to the dry leaves of memories, expectations, and desires to find relief? Because I am afraid of the alternative. I am like the man in the old joke, looking for his keys under the streetlamp rather than over by his car where he dropped them, because "the light is better here." Actually the light isn't better in the conditioned mind. It's just that the darkness is familiar and allows for a sense of control and containment.

My conditioned mind longs for forgiveness, yet fails to realize that it has been the architect of the prison of guilt and resentment in which it lives. But the key to this prison is also it its care. Willingness to step into the damp depths of the Tao Mind, even if for tiny moments at a time, will unlock the prison door. This key of willingness is all I need ask my conditioned mind to do. It can take this small step. Without this willingness, it will continue to sit in its cell and construct elaborate strategies and programs within itself in the hopes that they will provide release. They will not.

You and I are at this present moment (I am writing, you are reading) using our conditioned mind in an attempt to express and to understand this elusive thing we label "forgiveness." These words are our maps for the territory we want to explore. They are important, but imperfect. At this moment I am trying to express, with my conditioned words, that which I really cannot express. But this is the way of our human life together—we use the most helpful maps we can find to help us walk step by step through the territory of life. Let us not forget that only Tao Mind sees the territory "as it is." Though we rely upon and appreciate our maps, let's spend more and more of our time walking in and experiencing the territory itself.

My conditioned mind asks, "If forgiveness is more than my conditioned words, of what value are the words 'I'm sorry' and 'I forgive you'?"

Remember that words are important maps. They are not the territory, but they have the ability to make the exploration of the territory easier. When we say, "I'm sorry," and it emerges from the tenderness of our own open heart, the words can be a very accurate map by which others can catch a glimpse of the freedom of forgiveness. When the words "I forgive you" express that we have indeed released the resentment and anger in our hearts, the person who hears the words has the opportunity to release their own burdens surrounding the situation. When these words are attempts to make ourselves or others comply with expected politeness and do not emerge from the freedom of release, both the speaker and the hearer are likely to remain stuck. Words are not the thing itself, but if they arise from the Tao Mind, they are gateways to forgiveness.

Questions for Your Tao Mind

- *Why is it often so difficult to say, "I'm sorry"?*
- *Why is it often so difficult to say, "I forgive you"?*
- *Which, in general, is easier to say? Why?*

A Tao Mind Exercise

There are many rituals that help us move our attention to our Tao Mind. One of the oldest and most venerable of these is Tea. This exercise is an invitation to create your very own Tea Ceremony. Experiment with it and be open to the possibility that it may find a sacred place in your life.

• *Bring a pot of water to boil and have it ready to make your tea.*

• *Choose a tea blend that pleases you and that is available in a loose leaf form.*

• *Choose a cup whose texture and color helps you feel a sense of connection to simple, earthy things.*

• *Sit comfortably at a table or on a meditation cushion in a setting that is quiet and inviting.*

• *Take a pinch of the tea and hold it in the open palm of your hand. Feel the texture and notice the dry and brittle quality. Imagine that these leaves represent the resentment, disappointment, regret, or shame to which you are clinging.*

• *Take your time. Breathe quietly and see if you notice any reluctance that might arise. Ask yourself: Do I really want to immerse my feelings in the Tao? Do I truly desire them to be transformed into forgiveness, or do I want to keep them as they are?*

• *When you are ready, drop the leaves into the mug and pour the water.*

• *Let the leaves steep for four or five minutes and imagine the dry brittle feelings of guilt, shame, anger, or resentment being softened by the hot water, releasing forgiveness, understanding, acceptance, and compassion.*

• *Slowly, sip by sip, drink the tea. Imagine that you are drinking in the transformed feelings. Instead of shame, you taste tender acceptance. Instead of resentment, you take in empathy and compassion.*

- *When you near the end of the cup, notice the remains of the leaves. Imagine a sense of gratitude for the transformation of "dry and brittle" into moist and nourishing; guilt and anger into forgiveness and compassion.*
- *You might want to make a gentle bow to the tea equipment, allowing yourself to feel gratitude for the transformation process.*
- *Conclude the ceremony by mindfully washing the pot and cup and returning them to their place.*

A Tao Mind Meditation

Without the dry leaves there could be no tea.
I am willing to accept all that has happened.
Without the cup there could be no tea.
I am willing to drop my suffering into the cup.
Without the water there could be no tea.
I am willing to let my Tao Mind transform my pain.

Get out of the Boat!

Do I really want forgiveness?

A man once came to a Holy Woman, seeking a way to find forgiveness for his terrible mistakes. She instructed him to go to a nearby lake where he would find a boat. He was to get in the boat and row across the lake. On the other side he would find a beach and just beyond the beach he would find the forgiveness he sought.

He did as the Holy Woman said. When he got to the lake he found it larger and more forbidding than he had expected. He could not see the other side. But the boat was solid, comfortable, and loaded with provisions, so he got in and began to row.

He rowed all day and just as night was falling he finally came to the far shore. There was indeed a small beach there, but beyond the beach lay a forest, dark and dense. He was not going to go there at night so he stayed in the boat, just off the shore.

When morning came he was disappointed to see that the beach seemed even smaller and less hospitable than he remembered from the night before. The forest seemed even more forbidding as well. He sat all day in the boat wondering what to do. Finally he decided to ask the Holy Woman for clarification.

He rowed back across the lake and walked back to the Holy Woman's hermitage. "I saw no forgiveness on that shore. All I saw was a small beach and a dark forest," he whined. "What should I do?"

"You have to get out of the boat!" shouted the Holy Woman.

The man went off to find another person who might be able to help him find the forgiveness for which he so eagerly sought.

Conditioned mind is perfectly happy to adopt a spiritual practice of forgiveness. It would be glad to row a boat across a lake and back for a lifetime. What conditioned mind does not want to do, however, is to leave the boat behind and set foot on the territory itself.

All spiritual traditions were founded by people who had taken various boats, reached distant shores of freedom and joy, left the boats behind, and began to speak of that freedom and joy. The religions that tended to form around these people soon focused on the building and maintenance of boats. This was not a bad thing. A boat is helpful for crossing lakes. But the question always remains: Are we willing to leave the boat behind? (Tragically, many of these spiritual boats have become luxury liners, complete with such comfort and amenities that no one would even think of leaving them for unknown shores.)

Much of our social conditioning supports the idea of spiritual boats. "Boats are good for us," the story goes. "Everyone should have a boat to row. It is good exercise." But the Tao Mind sees boats, not as exercise, but as vehicles for reaching far shores.

The practice of forgiveness is a truly helpful boat. The idea of freeing another person or ourselves from the prison of guilt and resentment seems a good and virtuous thing. Conditioned mind is happy to set about the task of forgiveness. First it will decide exactly what forgiveness will be, how it will feel, and what things are necessary for it to be accomplished. It will create action steps, rituals, and words designed to bring it about. It will consider helpful ideas and even write helpful books. What it resists doing is stepping out of itself onto the shore of Tao Mind where forgiveness is actually experienced.

Do I really want to give forgiveness? Or do I want to make myself more comfortable while hanging on to my opinions, judgments, hurts, and righteous indignation? Do I want to receive forgiveness? Or do I want to be more comfortable while hanging on to my familiar feelings of being wrong, flawed, and inadequate? The honest answer for most of my sub-personalities is that I really want to keep my opinions and judgments about myself and others intact. But I want relief from the pain.

I am never going to convince a sub-personality who feels hurt and betrayed to feel otherwise, no matter how forceful and compelling the arguments might be. My only option is to step away from my conditioned mind (boat) into my Tao Mind. When I am able to do this, I see a different view of everything. The very sub-personality who is clinging to resentment and anger becomes a recipient of my compassion. "Poor thing—so hurt and angry." Once my own internal "selves" are accepted and forgiven for whatever they are experiencing, thinking, or feeling, the external situation is transformed. The compassion of the Tao Mind flows out from my own healed heart.

Questions for Your Tao Mind

- *Do you truly want to experience forgiveness? To give forgiveness?*
- *What "buts" arose when you answered the above questions?*

- *What about stepping out of the boat frightens you? What part of you is frightened? How old is this part? What does this part of you actually fear?*
- *What might you say or do to reassure this part of you?*

A Tao Mind Exercise

The step from the idea of forgiveness into the actual territory of forgiveness is not as difficult as our conditioning would have us believe. All it requires is a tiny amount of willingness, the kind of willingness that we exhibit when we take the next step in our day without knowing where we're going or how the day will turn out.

- *This is a walking exercise. Find an open space in your yard or in a room large enough for you to walk ten unobstructed paces.*
- *Stand comfortably and look around you to make sure nothing is in your way that would cause you to trip.*
- *Close your eyes and let your thoughts relax. Be willing to turn your attention to your Tao Mind. Don't try to define what that means. The willingness is all that is necessary.*

- *After a few moments, with your eyes still closed, take a step forward. Stop there and notice thoughts, sensations, and emotions.*
- *Still with eyes closed, take another step. Stop and notice.*
- *Continue taking steps with your eyes closed for as long as you are comfortable, stopping between steps to pay attention to everything that is going on in you.*
- *When you are no longer comfortable taking another step, open your eyes and notice where you are. Turn and notice where you have been.*
- *What do you notice about your own willingness to take a step, a small step, without knowing exactly where you are going?*

A Tao Mind Meditation

I do not want forgiveness,
I want to feel better.
I do not want to forgive,
I want things to be made right.
But I am willing to take one small step in the dark,
and then another.

The Mark of Cain

We are never outside the pale.

Cain and his younger brother, Abel, lived together in a small tribe of wandering hunters. The tribe had always cared for itself by hunting game and gathering wild plants. When the game and plants in a region grew scarce, the village would pack and move.

The brothers loved each other, but were often rivals in the way that most brothers are. Abel was the most accomplished hunter in the village and always brought back the most game. Cain was also a capable hunter but he had a secret dream, a dream that the village might one day be able to cultivate and grow their own crops, reseeding them each year and no longer having to migrate when food grew scarce.

Cain developed a detailed plan that he tried to explain to the village elders. They *scorned him and accused him of blasphemy, of not trusting their god to care for them as he always had. "You should be like your brother, Abel," they sneered. "He is a virtuous and intelligent hunter. Our god is pleased with him."*

Cain sat that evening at the edge of a meadow near the community's camp. He felt shame and anger. He kept reliving his presentation to the elders, wondering if he could have said something different or presented his plan in a clearer manner.

He was startled by his brother's voice from behind him. "Well, brother"—Abel laughed—"your great plan comes crashing down, huh? I told you it would."

Instantly, without thinking, Cain reached for a rock, rose, spun, and hurled it, all in one motion. The rock struck Abel on the forehead and killed him instantly. When Cain saw his brother's body crumpled on the ground, his heart froze. He could hardly catch his breath. Dozens of emotions spun through his mind—grief, shock, and finally, fear. He turned and ran into the wilderness, stumbling and falling, struggling to his feet and running on. He ran all night and finally collapsed by a creek and began to sob. He cried for a solid hour in grief, loss, and fear. He could not return to the tribe. The punishment would be banishment—to be cast out of the tribe to perish in the wilderness.

He stayed by the creek for several days, unable to eat, awaiting his fate. Small sips of water were all his churning stomach could keep down. Day and night his thoughts accused and tormented him—"Murderer! Evil! Your life is over! Kill your-

self!" These thoughts grew and grew until he began to think of finding a high cliff and throwing himself off of it just to silence them.

"I can't live with this guilt and this sorrow," he cried. "I can't!" Suddenly everything in his mind stopped—no thoughts, no feelings, nothing—just the awareness of his own breathing in the silence.

Then in the silence the Tao blew in the breeze and scuttled across the rocks in the sand, and Cain heard no more accusations. A small thought appeared in his mind that sounded quite different: "We can live with this," it said. "It will be very difficult but I will be with you and I will help you. It will not be easy, but a great blessing will come from your pain. I promise."

The moment faded away and the pain returned, but Cain was able to rise and go on. Eventually he came upon a large town, surrounded by fields of cultivated crops, exactly as he had hoped his own village might develop. He settled in that region and began to grow produce of his own on a small farm.

For two years he kept to himself, working his small farm and taking long walks. Gradually he began to smile more often at the people who came to market. For some reason, people who were troubled in their souls began to talk to him, sensing something in this quiet man that was receptive and accepting. He listened carefully to all who came to him and everyone found him to be a man who provided solace and comfort. He made a few close friends, people who knew and loved him. People often noticed tears in his eyes but the tears were accompanied by a soft smile that com-municated to people that, whatever they were experiencing, they were adequate for it—in fact he gave them hope that they would once again find happiness.

He would often be found taking long walks in the countryside by himself. As he walked people would notice that he seemed to be talking to himself—sometimes laughing, sometimes crying.

For generations to come, whenever a person was seen to have soft gentle eyes and a manner that welcomed and made space for everyone, this person was said to have "the mark of Cain."

There are times when our minds reel at the enormity of some action that our conditioned mind has conceived and carried out. We suddenly realize that we have caused real harm, have truly disrupted the lives of those we love, or have done that for which we feel a deep and secret shame. At these times, our social, and perhaps even biological, heritage often chooses exile—banishment—as the punishment. We have set ourselves outside the pale of decent people, the story goes, and we must forever wander in the wilderness of guilt and regret.

People in our lives will sometimes affirm this banishment, casting us out of a relationship, a marriage, or even sentencing us to prison. Even if our shame remains a secret, our own mind can drive us outside the community of love and acceptance, refusing to let us feel relief, forgiveness, or freedom, for we are seen by a part of our mind as unworthy.

But our Tao Mind is always ready to whisper in the gentle breeze that "this, too, can be integrated into life's intricate web. Those harmed and those who do the harm are each capable of using experience as the soil for wisdom." The old Irish concept of pale—a stake, or fence made of stakes, driven in the ground to mark a territory or sphere of authority—has no meaning in the Tao Mind. Nothing is "beyond the pale" of the Tao for its territory is the Cosmos—every atom of both the inner and the outer expressions of All That Is.

I hear my conditioned mind ask, "The death of another person by careless or thoughtless actions seems to be impossible to get over. Some apparently can do it, but how?"

This is a very painful question. My own fearful mind can easily paint a picture of my beloved spouse as the victim of a thoughtless or even cruel death. "What about that?" a very vicious part of my conditioning says. "Put that in your 'Tao Mind' and see what you get."

The Tao Mind would never ever ask us to "get over" the loss of a loved one. Instead it would invite us to discover the inherent courage of our own open heart. It would create a compassionate space where the memories could be visited in safety and tenderness rather than outrage and grief. We gradually discover that the open heart, though vulnerable and often subject to sadness, is an expression of our true nature, our Tao Mind. As our grief or shame is slowly turned into openhearted tenderness, forgiveness is the natural result. But great patience is required. Our hearts have been broken. Too easily saying "Get over it" or "Forgive" will only increase the pain of resistance. Healing comes from the inherent capacity waiting within us, not from forcing our broken subpersonalities to repress their pain.

As our own conditioned mind understands that it can never be "beyond the pale," it begins the difficult process of integration and growth. When this process is at work in a person we can truly see that "mark of Cain" in the tenderness, vulnerability, kindness, and compassion with which they approach the seeming outcasts of the world.

Questions for Your Tao Mind

- *What might it feel like to have committed a heinous crime?*
- *Are you willing to let tenderness and grace come from the worst thing you have ever done?*
- *Can anyone ever be "more evil" than the Tao Mind can accept?*

A Tao Mind Exercise

- *Sit quietly at a table with a pencil and a piece of white paper.*
- *Draw a circle in the middle of the paper and write your name in the middle of the circle.*
- *Let images of people or actions come to your mind that are completely "outside the pale"—totally unacceptable to you.*
- *Write these on the paper somewhere outside the circle.*
- *Are there any memories of actions of your own that go outside the circle?*
- *Are there any actions of people close to you that belong outside the circle?*
- *Sit for a moment and allow feelings and sensations to arise about "inside" and "outside."*
- *Let your attention shift to your Tao Mind. Sometimes it is helpful to move to a different place—a cushion or chair that helps you settle into that spacious mind.*
- *Pick one of the people or actions that is outside the pale. Can you see the potential for the "mark of Cain" to emerge from that person or situation?*
- *You will feel your conditioned mind saying, "That will never happen." Gently agree with your conditioned mind that, indeed, it probably won't*

happen. Then return to the Tao Mind and just imagine it happening. We can't control how other people respond to their actions. We can only sit with Tao Mind and see the possibility of wisdom and grace. That is enough.

A Tao Mind Meditation

(With apologies to the poet Edwin Markham, I borrow and edit for my purposes his famous lines.)

> *My mind calls me evil, a selfish lout*
> *and draws a circle that keeps me out.*
> *But Tao Mind has the wit to win.*
> *It draws a circle that takes me in.*
> *My mind calls them evil, selfish louts*
> *and draws a circle that keeps them out.*
> *But Tao Mind has the wit to win.*
> *It draws a circle that takes them in.*

There's No One in the Boat

We don't have to take it personally.

A man once took his canoe and set out at night to cross a large lake. It was a somewhat dangerous crossing to undertake in the dark, but he wanted to get to the other side by morning.

He paddled cautiously out into the calm waters. There was no moon. The sky was clouded over and a slight mist rose from the surface of the lake. He could hear nothing but the ripples lapping against the side of his canoe and the splash of his paddle as it entered and left the water. He could see no more than a few feet in either direction.

He had been paddling for about an hour and was beginning to feel tired. He sat back and rested his paddle across his knees for a moment. Suddenly he was thrown to the deck by a sharp impact against the side of the canoe. He nearly capsized and his heart beat rapidly as he regained his balance and looked up to see a motorboat resting against the side of his canoe where it had left a large dent.

He jumped to his feet and began waving his paddle about in the air and cursing at the top of his voice. How dare this idiot motorboat operator slam into him like this? How dare he be so careless? "You could have killed me, you moron!" he shouted. He received no reply and his anger increased. He was just about to climb into the motorboat and let the operator have a heavy swat from his paddle when his eyes focused through the mist and he realized that there was no one in the motorboat. It had drifted into him. No one was to blame.

Gradually his heartbeat began to slow and his anger to abate. The motorboat drifted away into the darkness and he was once again alone on the lake. He sat there for a while and finally began to chuckle. "There was no one in the boat," he thought. "I got so mad and there was no one to be mad at. There was no one in the boat!"

He began to paddle once more, when a sudden thought occurred to him. "There's no one in this boat either!" He began to laugh out loud as he continued his journey to the far side of the lake.

At this moment I am writing at the university library. I am in the "Quiet" section. There are signs everywhere that ask people to keep their cell phones turned off and not to engage in conversation. About fifteen feet from where I am sitting a young woman is carrying on a cell phone conversation in that typical just-below-a-shout tone that people use on cell phones. All of my attention is diverted toward her.

This is wrong.

She is wrong.

This should not be happening.

Someone should tell her to hang up.

Who does she think she is?

There is a sub-personality in me who is feeling all of the above as a whirling stir of energy. He is anxious and disturbed far beyond the actual content of the situation. He is taking this experience very personally. He is looking for a way to communicate to this person his annoyance because otherwise how will she know she is "wrong"? She finally finishes her conversation and walks away without looking in my direction and getting the glare she so richly deserves.

Isn't that interesting? This angry, stirred-up part of me is someone who has always been told to "be good, be nice, be unobtrusive, obey all the rules or you will not be acceptable." When he senses "rule-breaking" occurring, he internalizes it as a personal threat. But "there is no one in the boat." The young woman is now sitting at a table quietly studying. I can now see that she tried to go to an area of the library that was as unobtrusive as possible to answer her phone.

"But," my rule-keeping self insists, "she should not have had her phone on in the first place. That's against the rules!" Poor little fellow, this part of me will always be threatened by any behavior that he perceives as outside the bounds of how-we're-supposed-to-be. I am now viewing him with a sense of compassion and sympathy. Of course he gets upset. He was thoroughly trained in "good" behavior and truly feels his safety depends on such behavior.

Much of the suffering that we work with in the practice of forgiveness arises from the conditioned mind's habit of taking everything personally. In one sense, of course, my life is very "personal." Each of my sub-personalities has the perspective that what happens to them is happening to "me." "This is my life," they say. Things don't get much more personal than that. Therefore, when something or someone from outside my skin acts in such a way as to threaten my safety, thwart my desires, hurt my feelings, ignore my wants, or in any of a thousand ways seems to impinge on "my" life, I take it very personally—at least the "I" of whatever sub-personality is present at the time takes it very personally.

Notice that the same conditioning that sorts external events and people into "right" and "wrong" is also ever-vigilant in its scrutiny of our own actions, moods, and thoughts. The myth it promotes is that, without such scrutiny, we would disintegrate into a chaotic, irresponsible, and destructive mess (just like the world it sees outside). This is not the way of the Tao Mind. The Tao Mind is open and accepting, deeply personal, yet not taking things personally. In the presence of such spaciousness, a natural and flexible effectiveness is enabled. Effective and correct action occurs because it arises naturally from a place of clarity and openness, not because strict scrutiny has been applied.

Questions for Your Tao Mind

- *Are you holding on to a sense that something that has happened is, indeed, very personal?*
- *What benefit do you gain from seeing this as personal?*
- *Is there some benefit in feeling "wronged"?*
- *Is there some benefit in feeling "guilty"?*

A Tao Mind Exercise

- *Allow yourself to sit in a relaxed yet alert posture.*
- *Take five relaxed, full breaths.*
- *Allow your mind to drift to a recent occasion of irritation, of taking the words and actions of another person personally. It could be something as simple as having to wait in line at the market, or being cut off in traffic.*
- *Notice the voices in your mind that insist that this was personal. They will present compelling reasons for their opinion.*
- *Once you have a sense of the "personal" feelings of this part of you, stand and stretch, reaching your hands toward the sky as far as you can. Hold this stretch as you count slowly to ten.*
- *Lower your arms and shake your hands at the wrists—with vigor—for a few seconds.*
- *Sit back down and relax. Can you sense a place in your mind where this occasion is not seen in a personal manner? If you can't glimpse this place, don't worry. We're just practicing opening up the possibility. That is enough.*
- *Take five more relaxed breaths and go about your day.*

A Tao Mind Meditation

There is no one in the boat.
It seems so personal and hurts so much,
someone must be wrong.
But, there is no one in the boat.
I am not here to be right
and make other people wrong.
I am here to pay attention
and let my Tao Mind show the way.
There is no one in the boat.

The Scapegoat

There is no need for blame.

Long ago, a nomadic people living in a vast wilderness region of the world would tell themselves frightening stories about the anger and punishment that the gods would mete out whenever they were displeased. These people interpreted any of the natural disasters, illnesses, misfortunes, and losses that are naturally a part of Life in the Tao as special punishments given because they had somehow not been good enough, proper enough, or that they had not believed or said the right things.

In an attempt to atone for their faults they devised an elaborate ritual designed to show their repentance. The leaders of the people would lay their hands on a goat and symbolically transfer the transgressions of the people onto the goat. This goat was called the Scapegoat. The goat would then be driven alone into the wilderness to die. Should the goat accidentally wander back into camp, it would be killed immediately.

One small goat was chosen to be this year's Scapegoat. He was terribly frightened when the people shouted and threw rocks at him to drive him away. He ran through the darkness until he was so tired he could run no farther and stood, panting, waiting for whatever wild animal would be his fate. But instead of a wild animal, he heard a kindly voice speak to him. "You look tired and hungry. Come with me and I'll give you food and rest."

The Scapegoat turned and saw a man standing with a staff in his hand. The man turned and began to walk away, stopped, looked back, and said, "Well, come along." The goat followed cautiously, too tired and hopeless to think of anything else to do. After walking a short time they came to a small campsite with a blazing fire where several other men and women were sitting. Just beyond the fire was a large herd of goats, including two of his friends who had been Scapegoats in earlier years.

The man said, "These are the Scapegoats who have been driven out in past years. As long as people are afraid to look deeply into themselves and to accept both the helpful and harmful qualities they find there, they will blame the gods and other people and they will always find scapegoats. Until they are willing to face their fears, I and my descendants will remain here to care for these scapegoats. Go, join them. There is food and warmth waiting for you."

The young goat ran, bleating in relief and joy, to join his herd.

Our conditioned mind finds emotional comfort in the process of making "scapegoats" out of people, families, groups, political parties, nations, and more often than not, out of some part of itself. The complexity of the cosmos and of human society makes it impossible to understand, much less to control, the myriad events that impinge on our lives. We want to blame someone because to blame implies that we understand what happened well enough to assign that blame. This gives us some illusion of control.

But blame is impossible to assign with any assurance. Wars, economic downturns, accidents, illnesses—all of the tragic, uncontrollable losses and pains of life are beyond our ability to understand, therefore to accurately assign blame. But—we do it anyway. We create scapegoats. It is one of our ways of coping with the uncomfortable mystery of life.

A part of our being knows that creating scapegoats does not actually explain or solve our difficulties. Republicans/Democrats (take your pick) are not truly the source of all evil. But our conditioned mind does not feel comfortable until someone or something carries the blame for that which is beyond our control.

Of course, the process of creating an external scapegoat merely mirrors the process occurring within our own minds. Somewhere, deep within our psyche, a very young sub-personality is being told that, in some manner that no one can quite explain, this is all his fault. He believes this story and begins to carry the blame. This hidden shame becomes a burden that he must carry in silence, never mentioning it in the polite company of the conditioned mind. We cannot let the scapegoat back into the camp of consciousness.

External scapegoats are mirrors of this internal process. As long as we have them out there, we will continue to carry them inside. As long as they are inside, we will project them out onto others. Tao Mind waits to rescue these little ones and give them comfort and rest, to remove the burden from their back and welcome them to a life of freedom.

As usual, our conditioned mind poses a question: "Are not some people actually 'to blame' for some things—drunk drivers who kill children, for instance?"

Each of us bears a sense of responsibility for the consequences of our actions. We act and consequences ensue. A big part of the practice of the Tao of Forgiveness is a practice of learning to live in a spacious and tender manner with this responsibility. We are all capable of this task. We are all "response-able"—

able to handle the consequences of success and honor, or failure and shame, from the courage and forgiveness of our Tao Mind. Blame, however, is quite another story. It is the outgrowth of need to feel in control of life. It keeps us in a tight trap of clinging to the stories we tell ourselves of how "this shouldn't have happened," and "if only I [they] had acted differently."

Questions for Your Tao Mind

- *Can you sense the difference in your emotions and bodily sensations when you say, "He is to blame," versus when you say, "He is responsible"?*
- *How about the difference between "I am to blame" and "I am responsible"?*

A Tao Mind Exercise

Whenever we say, "If only I had done [or not done] . . ." we are creating a scapegoat. Someone within us is being asked to carry a burden for the rest of his life. We have set up a relationship in our mind in which one part of us assigns blame and another part carries that blame.

• *The difference between these two "voices" is sometime hard to see. Let your attention rest on your breath as it enters and leaves the body.*

• *Let your memory mind rest on a feeling of blame. Be very attentive and see if you can get an image of "who" is blaming and "who" is being blamed.*

• *On a plain sheet of paper, draw two simple figures representing these two voices. (I know, you hate to draw. We can work on that self-blame later.) Just draw simple representations that no one else will ever see.*

• *What do you see? What do you feel?*

• *Turn your attention to the one assigning the blame. How old is this one? Listen carefully to him and do not blame him for his feelings of blame. What does he need from you?*

• *Turn your attention to the one carrying the blame. How old is this one? What is he hearing about himself? What does he need from you?*

• *What would a spacious, generous part of your Tao Mind say to each of these two that might ease their suffering?*

A Tao Mind Meditation

In my mind are many scapegoats
carrying burdens far too heavy
for little ones to bear.
I drive them out
and lay the burdens on others,
but they find their way back
in the dark of night.
I make a campfire to warm them
and prepare food for them to eat.
I vow to end their suffering,
thereby ending mine.

The Suffering of Sisyphus

Burdens can be laid down.

Sisyphus strained his back against the all-too-familiar weight of the boulder. He knew, by now, every crack and crevasse, every variation of texture, every uneven surface of the boulder that was his to push up the mountain. He also knew every step of the steep path up the mountain that marked his journey. He would push this boulder up the mountain until he reached the top. Once at the top there was no place the boulder could rest and it would roll down the mountain, all the way to the valley where the journey had begun and his toil would begin once again.

One day Sisyphus descended the mountain and found an old man leaning against the boulder, looking at him with a sad smile.

"Who are you?" Sisyphus asked the man.

"A friend," the old man said. "Why are you pushing this boulder up the hill?"

"It is what I have to do," replied Sisyphus. "I am being punished for my arrogance, pride, and sinfulness. But once I can get the boulder to remain on the top of the mountain, I will be free."

"I see," said the old man. "And is there a place for the boulder to rest on top of the mountain?"

"I haven't found one yet," admitted Sisyphus.

"I see," said the old man.

Sisyphus stood quietly for a moment. Then he turned and put his shoulder to the boulder and started back up the mountain. As he pushed and shoved his load over the rocky path he thought about the countless times he had repeated this process, always hoping that this time would be the last, that the boulder would find a resting place and he would be free.

When he reached the top he looked around with a new clarity. The top of the mountain was solid rock and the peak was far too small for the boulder to balance firmly.

"It will always roll back down," he thought. At that moment the boulder slipped away and began its journey crashing and tumbling back down the mountain.

Slowly Sisyphus made his way back, his mind filled with clarity and despair. When he reached the bottom he found the old man once again leaning against the boulder.

"Well?" said the old man.

"There is no place the boulder will rest," Sisyphus cried. "I will never be free."

The old man took Sisyphus by the arm, gently pulled him to one side, and said, "You know, this valley is quite beautiful, isn't it? Walk with me for a while and we'll enjoy each other's company." Sisyphus looked around. Indeed the valley was lush and inviting, filled with fields and streams and forests. He took a deep breath of clean, fresh air. He stretched his arms and, for a moment, enjoyed the sights and aromas. Then, suddenly, his shoulders slumped and he turned back to the boulder. Before he began his endless trek he asked the old man, "What is your name?"

"My name is Freedom," said the man.

"Will I see you again?" said Sisyphus over his shoulder as he began to push the boulder.

"Every time you come down the mountain," said the man.

I live in a beautiful Northern California town that is surrounded by a large, fertile valley. A farmer's market operates all year round, offering an amazing variety of produce in every season. I have interesting work to do and I do it in the midst of people who are warm and loving. I am married to a beautiful spouse who loves me, accepts me as I am, and sees me very much with her Tao Mind. Why in the world would I keep putting my shoulder to the boulder and pushing it up a barren mountain?

Because my conditioned mind, bless its heart, still believes that self-punishment is the path to self-improvement. It sounds oh-so-convincing when it suggests, "Unless I discipline you [it avoids the actual word "punishment"], you will not be motivated to improve." It has been doing this for years and the full weight of society seems to back up its case. No one ever seems to notice that the boulder will never stay on top of the mountain. We continue to believe the promise: "This time we'll get it to stay."

Conditioned mind protests, "What's wrong with a little self-discipline? It has worked pretty well for me. I would not be the success I am today without it."

Notice how easily we interchange the words "self-discipline" and "self-punishment." The root meaning of "discipline" implies an eager willingness to study, work, and persevere because we are devoted to the task; because the activity brings satisfaction and meaning to an authentic part of our nature. "Self-punishment" is a different process entirely. It can masquerade as self-discipline but we can catch the important difference if we pay attention.

Punishment always implies that we are somehow "wrong," and if left to our own devices we will remain, or even become, more deeply "wrong." So we punish with words and actions for the stated goal of: "So that we might learn better." But the unstated truth of the punishment process is that we will never learn better. This process is self-perpetuating. It will keep itself alive by any means possible. It keeps us feeling "wrong," so "wrongness" will always be the filter through which we see ourselves and our actions. Therefore punishment will always be necessary. We remain trapped in the classic "The beatings will continue until morale improves" school of life.

Notice carefully how true self-discipline feels. See if you can catch the difference in the internal tone of voice between the two processes. The Tao Mind understands the freedom of true discipline—a joyful pursuit of a natural path. The conditioned mind tends to fall back on self-punishment—the narrow pursuit of an unattainable "should do" or "should be."

How fortunate we all are that our Tao Mind sits waiting at the bottom of the hill, always ready to provide the fellowship of freedom. That we so often turn back to our burden is not a failing on our part; it is merely a mental habit that we will one day lay down. We have been deeply conditioned to push the boulder. It will take practice to remain in the valley of freedom. Perhaps the next time down the mountain we will remain for a bit longer in freedom's presence.

Questions for Your Tao Mind

- Why might you be unwilling to accept forgiveness that is freely and openly available to you?
- What mountain are you trying to push a boulder up right now? Do you really need to?

A Tao Mind Exercise

- Locate a reasonably heavy rock—not so heavy that it will strain your back, but substantial enough for you to feel its weight when you carry it—twenty pounds or so. Any weighty object will do if you can't find a rock, but I like the rock because of its natural symbolic qualities.
- Lay out a short path in your yard and place the stone at one end of the path.
- Stand by the stone for a few moments and let your breath be relaxed and full.
- Pick up the stone (be careful of your back—don't make the stone that heavy).
- Walk slowly with the stone to the other end of the path and carefully lay it down.

- *Stand for a few moments by the stone and watch the sensations and emotions that arise, then mindfully pick up the stone again and walk back to the start.*
- *Repeat until you have a sense of modest fatigue and an awareness of what the physical acts of "putting down" and "picking up" feel like in your body.*
- *I suggest this meditation as a practice when you feel burdened by a forgiveness issue. You might want to recite the meditation verse from this chapter as you lift, carry, and lay down the stone. The verse can also be used whenever you notice that you have, once again, picked up some thought habit that you might want to lay back down.*

A Tao Mind Meditation

Picking up this burden, I am aware of picking it up.
Walking with this burden, I can feel its weight.
Laying it down, I notice the relaxation and relief.
Shall I pick it back up?

If I do, when shall I lay it down again?
Who is telling me to carry it?
Is that true?
What would I do if I could lay it down?
Who might I be?

The Snarl of Yarn

Memories can be a tapestry of compassion.

A very young boy was taking a walk in the woods with his father when he spied a bright blue piece of yarn hanging on the leaves of a forest fern. Delighted, he picked the yarn from the fern and stuffed it in his pocket. A bit farther along he saw a longer piece of red yarn dangling from a twig. He put this in his pocket as well.

From then on, every time he would go outdoors he would be on the lookout for additions to his yarn collection. By the time he was a young man he had a large ball of yarn, knotted and snarled together, that he carried in his backpack wherever he went. It was composed of all colors—some bright and cheerful, some plain and ordinary. He was actually beginning to get tired of the massive ball, but he couldn't seem to stop picking up threads of yarn wherever he found them.

By the time he reached middle age he had to wheel the ball in a large cart. It made traveling inconvenient and tiring, but still he kept adding the threads he found each day. One evening, as he sat contemplating the ball, he had the glimmer of an idea.

He sat down by the ball and began to gently unravel one of the threads, then he unraveled another, and another. When he had about twenty threads of various colors and lengths, he took them to his loom and began to weave them together. Each evening he would sit down and patiently unravel and unknot a few threads and weave them onto the tapestry that was taking shape on his loom. Some evenings he had to be content with just loosening some of the knots a bit, so tightly snarled were they. Other evenings he found that some threads came loose easily and he could add them to his growing tapestry.

The threads he would continue to find each day were added directly to the weaving rather than the ball. Gradually, over the span of several years, the ball was transformed into a large and lovely tapestry.

One day he untied the last knot and with great joy wove the last thread into the tapestry. He carefully removed it from the loom and took it over to the wall. He hung it so he could look at it from any vantage point in his house, even through the open door of his bedroom so it would be the first thing he would see when he woke up.

The years passed and he grew old, yet still each day he would find new threads and bring them home to add to the bottom of the tapestry. Each evening he would rest and enjoy the beauty of his weaving. One evening, on his way home, he saw a lovely lustrous black thread, unlike any he had seen before. "This will be perfect for the bottom of my hanging," he thought. He brought the thread home and carefully wove it. It seemed to just fit along the bottom of the weaving. As he finished, he felt quite tired and sat back in his chair. He looked at his tapestry with a sense of satisfaction. The sense of pleasant tiredness grew and he closed his eyes. His last sight was of the tapestry. His last thought was "How beautiful it is."

The Tao presents multicolored moments like threads caught on bushes waiting to be collected by someone passing by. Our conditioned mind has the habit of grabbing such moments without thought and cramming them into the snarl of our habitual patterns.

Moments that could be woven with care and mindfulness into our own unique tapestry of life are too often tangled together in a conditioned set of reactions and responses. Joys and sorrows, satisfactions and disappointments, achievements and failures are held tightly in a wad of memories. This confusing and unconscious ball is then used by conditioned mind to narrow and limit our experience and our perspective.

Each new moment, each unique thread of life, passes from direct experience into the ball of memories so quickly that its color and texture goes unnoticed. It becomes wadded rather than woven, and life becomes a snarl instead of a tapestry.

Perhaps the most difficult threads to weave are those whose appearance makes the conditioned mind uncomfortable. You know them—threads of embarrassment, guilt, shame, regret, anger, disappointment, and resentment—the threads that are the content of our practice of forgiveness. It sometimes seems easier to stuff such experiences into the ball and forget them. But of course we don't forget them. They join the semiconscious chorus that dominates and directs our life.

Regrets may have plagued us for decades. Perhaps our conditioned mind has kept certain stories on replay for so long that the awareness of them has subsided into the unconscious. There they remain, playing over and over. We do not want to undertake a practice that brings them into the open because we feel it would be just too much for us to handle. Better to keep them somewhat under wraps and continue the accommodation we have made with them—they will remain hidden and we will continue to listen and believe, and suffer.

When we finally realize that nothing short of a plunge into that which we have been avoiding all our lives will do, we find the willingness to practice—to begin an exploration of our own mind and the ways in which it has conditioned our life. Gently and gradually we unravel first this tiny thread and then that one. Eventually a small knot comes undone and our life opens to a bit more acceptance, a bit more spaciousness. We come to understand this piece of conditioning that has held in place a belief that no longer serves us. We let it go, sigh in relief, and turn with renewed hope to the next knot—a bigger one this time! One thread at a time we do our work. Each one loosened now is available for the tapestry of wisdom instead of the snarl of conditioning. That which held suffering in place now supports joy. The threads remain the same but the experience is transformed.

A few days ago I was driving home in a preoccupied mood. As I turned from the street that ran alongside the park onto a main north-south road, I almost hit a bicyclist who was approaching on the wrong side of the road. As he quickly stopped his bike, he fell over to one side. He was clearly "wrong" and I was first startled, then frightened, then angry—a typical pattern for the unfolding of emotions.

I pulled over to make sure he was okay. He got up and walked to my car, cursing. I responded by pointing out that he was riding on the wrong side of the road—wrong, wrong, wrong! We exchanged angry words and I told him to call the police if he felt he had been wronged. He calmed down a bit. I calmed down a bit. We agreed that no damage had been done, shook hands, and went on our way.

End of story? Of course not. My conditioning spent the next several hours replaying the event, helpfully suggesting ways I could have handled the incident "better." Do any of these have a familiar ring?

"You're a Zen teacher, for crying out loud! You should have been serene, gentle, and calm."

"You're a wimp. You should have beat the crap out of the jerk."

"If you had been mindful you would have seen him, wrong side of the road or not."

"He's probably going to track you down and kill you."

All of these, plus several dozen variations, became the focus of my distracted attention. Finally I turned to my Tao Mind.

"Interesting," smiled Tao Mind. I began to look at the whole incident without judgment for either the cyclist or for myself. It became simply an event in the tapestry of the day. The various sub-personalities who dominated the event—the angry rebel, the frightened little kid, the aggressive boundary-keeper—were all seen without criticism.

"Yep," said Tao Mind, "that's what happened all right." I asked for wise and helpful suggestions. My Tao Mind laughed. "I don't make 'helpful' suggestions.

Any learning that comes from the event will happen naturally as you see it without attachment and judgment.'"

Will I get hooked again in similar circumstances? Possibly. Is there a somewhat greater chance that I will have increased mindfulness and be less likely a victim of sub-personality takeover? Probably. The incident has taken its place as a thread woven into a tapestry of memories. It is not part of the snarl. Forgiveness? It is an unavoidable by-product of the weaving.

Questions for Your Tao Mind

- *How accurate are your memories?*
- *Are there memories to which you constantly return? Why?*
- *How do memories hinder forgiveness?*

A Tao Mind Exercise

This exercise is practice in the willingness to look at one thread at a time instead of at the whole knotted-up ball.

- *Sit comfortably with your journal.*
- *Let your mind rest and drift until you notice an uncomfortable train of thought—shame, anger, regret, disappointment, etc.*
- *Shift your attention to the memory of the incident that seems to be central.*
- *The moment your mind begins to tell you what this "means" about you or others, shift back to the mere details of the event itself, even though they may be painful.*
- *Notice how the pain increases as the mind once again begins to tell you what this "means."*
- *Describe the incident in your journal in nonjudgmental terms. This is difficult. Notice the tendency to use subtle judgments in your description. Stick to: This or that happened; He or she said; They did; etc. It may help if you refer to your own words and actions in the third person—"Bill said . . ."*
- *Is there a part of your mind that is unwilling to give up the judgments? It may be interesting to shift your attention to this part—not the judgments, but the feelings. "What do you feel? What do you need? To what are you clinging?"*
- *You are practicing seeing the event and people in neutral terms—the "just what happened," not the why it happened or what it means. This is the thread that Tao Mind can weave into the tapestry of your life.*

• *I realize that this is very difficult. Some events are so traumatic and seen with such loss, guilt, regret, and anger that a nonjudgmental view seems impossible. Don't worry if you have difficulty. You don't have to change anything. We're just nurturing our tiny bit of willingness to live in freedom—one step, one moment, at a time.*

A Tao Mind Meditation

Am I my memories?
Or am I the one who weaves the memories?
Can I find a place for the painful ones in my tapestry?
I don't want to see clearly.
Keeping my thoughts confused, entangled, and snarled
protects me from the pain of clarity.
But I am willing.
I can see one small memory
without judgment.
Perhaps tomorrow I can see another.

The Birds

_____

Conditioned voices fade away.

Stanley was cursed by a large flock of raucous, chattering birds. For some reason this flock of birds had attached themselves to Stanley and followed him wherever he traveled. At night, they sat on the eaves of his house and squawked and twittered from dusk until dawn. When he walked out of the house in the morning they flew a short distance into the air and remained circling above his head throughout the day. He tried throwing rocks, yelling, waving his arms wildly—nothing worked. The birds remained as if they were attached by string to his head.

Stanley went to the Taoist Sage who lived in a neighboring village. "I am cursed by birds," he wailed above the cheeping and tweeting. "Please help me get rid of them."

The Sage looked calmly at the birds. "Everyone has birds," he said. "You can't get rid of them."

"Can't get rid of them!" cried Stanley. "Oh my God, I'll go crazy. I can't live with all this noise."

"Walk with me," said the Sage, and they walked for several hours up over a small mountain range and down the other side to the ocean. They made their way down a steep path cut into the cliff until they reached an expanse of sandy beach.

Together, they walked out to the ocean's edge and stood looking across the vast water to the horizon.

"Now what?" said Stanley, whose birds continued to circle close over his head.

"Now, nothing," said the Sage. "Just listen to the ocean."

Stanly tried. At first all he was aware of was the familiar chattering of high-pitched bird squawks, but for a moment he did notice the background rhythmic gentle washing of the endless waves against the shore. As he turned his attention to the sound, the birds about his head began to circle a few feet higher. When he turned his attention back, the circle of birds tightened back down.

He turned his attention back to the ocean and, once again, the birds expanded their range, circling even farther away this time.

He turned to the Sage. "Interesting," Stanley said.

The Sage nodded. "The ocean is your Tao Mind. It is always there, always offering an infinite amount of room for your life. Do you understand?"

"I don't know," said Stanley, "but I want to be here by the ocean more often, that's for sure."

The Sage smiled. "It is always here."

"By the way," said Stanley, "you said everyone has birds. Where are yours?"

"Oh," said the Sage with a dismissive wave of his hand, "they're still here but their circle is miles away. I hardly notice them anymore unless I really concentrate on them. And I can't imagine why I would want to do that, can you?"

Our conditioned mind would like to present the chattering of our internal voices as Real Life. It would suggest that we have no alternative but to pay attention to the constant cacophony and try, somehow, to make sense out of it, to somehow take guidance from all of the contradictory, illogical, and frightening noises.

Among the many birds that clamor for our attention are resentment, disappointment, anger, guilt, shame, judgment, and the rest of the voices associated with our practice of forgiveness. In one sense it is helpful to pay attention to these voices, finding out how they arise and how they manage to capture our attention in such a way as to keep themselves in tight little circles about our head. But as we do this practice it will be essential to keep the ocean in mind. The Tao Mind is the background of spacious acceptance that allows this practice of forgiveness to be possible. Trying to do this practice from conditioned mind alone would be like trying to get rid of the birds by putting out a daily ration of birdseed. We want to watch them, accept them, understand them, but not feed them. We cannot think our way out of our suffering by using the same thinking that created it. We must practice diligently at using a different mind altogether.

It might be helpful to define "attention" as that part of our mind that selects, from the array of sensory and mental input available in a particular moment, that which we will admit to our consciousness as "what's happening." As we practice moving into the freedom of forgiveness, we will be learning to decide just where we want our attention to rest—with the birds of our conditioned mind, or with the spaciousness of our Tao Mind.

When there is a job to do or a problem to solve our attention can naturally turn to the details. This is the blessing of the conditioned mind. If we can attend to the task at hand while still remaining aware of the background ocean of Tao Mind, we will be living in a natural effectiveness and freedom.

However, the birds of our conditioned mind love to circle and look for food. These "birds of thought" will readily feed on the things that keep forgiveness from entering our life—resentment, anger, blame, shame, and guilt. These things have a lot of mental energy and the mental pathways they create are well-traveled and easy to follow. Practicing forgiveness is a patient process of noticing when our attention is focused on these things, then gently and compassionately turning it to the broader background of our life—to the ocean of Tao in which we swim. Each time we turn our attention in this manner, we are creating new pathways that will gradually become easier to follow. Remember that forgiveness is a natural part of this Tao Mind and is always there waiting when we no longer turn our attention to the cheeping and cawing that keep resentment and guilt alive.

Questions for Your Tao Mind

- *Where does your attention normally rest?*
- *Are you always turning your conscious mind to the issues, beliefs, and stories that keep you from forgiveness?*
- *How do the countless distractions of our society give the illusion of rest while*

still keeping our attention away from the ocean of Tao Mind, keeping us unconscious of the forgiveness waiting there?

A Tao Mind Exercise

This exercise is simple and basic to our practice. It is simply taking a moment to bring your attention to your breathing. Few of us live near the ocean, but we all live in intimacy with our breath.

- *Take a moment and let your attention gradually find its way to the way your breath is entering and leaving your body.*
- *You don't have to do this for an extended period of time, just a minute or so is sufficient to give yourself a glimpse of the spaciousness that is always available to you.*
- *I would guess that, as you put your attention on your breath, the noises and voices in your mind have continued. This is fine. It may take quite a while before the circle of bird noise begins to move a noticeable distance away for any length of time. We're looking for just a brief sense of expansion.*

- *Notice if any of these noises and voices are tied to guilt, shame, anger, resentment, or blame.*
- *Return your attention once more to your breath. Imagine the subtle sensation and sound of it is the distant song of the ocean, wave after wave coming to the shore, then receding. When you are aware of your breath alone, you are in the presence of Tao Mind—that simple. (And, of course, that difficult.)*

A Tao Mind Meditation

The birds are familiar and noisy.
They clamor for attention,
distract, and divert me from my life.
They accuse me of transgressions
and point out the evil others do.
I have created them
and I accept them.
But I choose not to feed them.
May their noise become faint in the distance
and the soothing surf of the Tao be my company.

The Lost Shovel

Projection creates reality.

Gerald was an avid gardener. His backyard was the envy of the neighborhood, and his vegetable garden produced enough tomatoes, beans, and squash to keep minestrone soup on the neighbors' dinner tables for several blocks around.

Of course such a garden required hours of hard work, especially in soil preparation. Gerald was an expert at soil preparation. His compost pile was scientifically designed and he was constantly using his favorite shovel to turn the rich compost into the soil. He kept this shovel clean and sharp, taking care that it didn't rust or chip. Holding this shovel in his hands made Gerald feel like a real "Gardener."

One morning he went to his toolshed and found an empty space where the shovel usually hung. Frantically Gerald searched the shed, the yard, the car, and even in-

side the house—no shovel. He always hung it up each evening. He never misplaced it. He concluded that someone must have entered the toolshed and stolen it.

That afternoon the young neighbor boy walked by and called his usual cheerful greeting to Gerald. Gerald had always considered the boy to be a pleasant and capable youngster, helpful and courteous. But today, as the boy whistled to himself as he continued down the street, Gerald watched him with a growing unease. Was he hurrying a bit more than usual? Did he glance back over his shoulder? He never does that. Is he hiding something?

As the days passed and Gerald made do with a replacement shovel, his suspicions grew and he resolved to keep a careful eye on the boy. When the boy would walk by, Gerald would scrutinize him carefully, watching for any telltale sign of guilt. Sure enough, the boy began to look more and more evasive under Gerald's stern glare. Eventually he stopped greeting Gerald and kept his eyes averted as Gerald continued to watch his every move. Finally the boy stopped coming by altogether.

"It is as clear as day," Gerald said to his wife one evening, "that boy is guilty. You can see it in his eyes. You can hear it in his voice." Whenever he saw the boy his opinion was reinforced. Anyone could see that the boy was headed for trouble.

One evening Gerald began the task of turning over his compost pile, bringing the decayed matter from the bottom up to the top. As his pitchfork plunged into the bottom layer, he heard a clunk. *Pushing the compost aside, Gerald reached down and picked up his precious shovel. It had fallen into the pile and been covered over with autumn leaves.*

Delighted with his discovery, Gerald headed for the garage to get a rag and some oil to clean the shovel. He looked up to see the neighbor boy pass by on the other side of the street. "What a nice boy," Gerald thought. "Anyone can see that he is headed for a good life. I wonder why he doesn't come around anymore?"

A cinema projector literally casts an image onto a blank screen. When we sit in a darkened theater with the movie playing we do not see the screen, we see the images projected upon it. They are "real" to us and the screen is merely a vehicle by which we see them. So it is with our inner life—we see it and make it real by projecting it onto the world around us.

It is very difficult to see other people just as they are. We are constantly projecting a variety of dramas, comedies, and adventures onto them and these projections often seem more "real" to us than the people themselves. We think we see them, know them, and understand them but all we really know is our projection.

Sometimes projections can contain a touch of accuracy. I may project love and affection onto the actions of my spouse and she would agree that, indeed, she feels loving and affectionate toward me at that time. In this case, my projection is accurate but it remains a projection. It remains an experience viewed through the lens of my own conditioned mind.

There is nothing wrong with projection. It is the way our brain makes sense of the outer world—comparing the sensory inputs it receives with existing categories it has stored and forming a sense of coherent meaning from all of the people, events, and feelings it is presented with. We don't really want to stop our mind from doing this. We will be much happier, however, if we are aware that this is what we are doing. Awareness allows us to hold our opinions, judgments, and conclusions with a certain lightness that keeps us balanced. In a dark theater we can become immersed in the images being projected to such a degree that our emotions, mental patterns, and physical reactions are affected just as if the images we were seeing were *real*. When the film ends it takes a few moments to return to an awareness that this *didn't really happen*. A large segment of my mind and body hasn't made the distinction.

In the realm of our own projections it is much more difficult to make the distinction. Decades of conditioning have led us to believe that any meaning we attach to a situation is completely and unalterably what is actually happening. No wonder we have trouble letting go of resentment and judgment.

The film *Indiana Jones and the Crystal Skull* contains a vivid expression of projection. The hero, Indiana Jones, is being sucked into a pit of quicksand. The only thing his comrades can find to throw to him is a huge, twenty-foot-long rat snake. The snake is harmless and apparently (remember, this is a *movie*) strong enough to be used as a rope by which they can pull him out of the pit.

But our hero has a weakness. He is terrified of snakes. He cannot bring himself to grab the snake when they throw it to him, even though he is now up to his armpits in the sand. His companions continue to scream, "Grab the snake!" Indiana screams, "Don't call it a snake. Call it a rope!" Finally his rescuers relent and yell, "Grab the rope." He grabs the snake's body and they pull him from the pit.

When I find myself holding on to a resentment, grudge, or judgment, it is helpful for me to remember two things: (1) It is a sub-personality, a conditioned part of my ego-identity, that is doing the holding on, and (2) This sub-personality is viewing things through the lens of his own projector. If I can switch my attention to my Tao Mind I am able to touch a feeling of release and relief. The projections begin to fade. The person and the situation become viewed with more clarity.

This does not mean that everything becomes calm and serene. I may be in a situation where a person *is* causing, or trying to cause, me harm. I may indeed need to take action, even vigorous action, to protect myself and my needs. But in this case my action arises from the clarity of a Tao Mind perspective. Such action is clean, concise, and leaves no residue of judgment.

Questions for Your Tao Mind

- *A friend once said to me, "It is safer to assume that everything is a snake until I find out otherwise." Are you more inclined to assume "snake"—or are you more inclined to assume "rope"?*
- *If you assume all external situations are "snakes," what do you assume about yourself—your own essential nature?*
- *Is there another option? What about not assuming anything?*

A Tao Mind Exercise

The conditioned mind is amazingly clever. It can turn a snake into a rope. It can also turn a rope into a snake if it is glimpsed in the shadows along a desert trail. In the following exercise you have the opportunity to play with your imagination to get some awareness of how the mind creates its projections.

- *Find a length of rope about three feet long and coil it loosely on the table in front of you.*
- *Sit quietly and close your eyes. Count your breath for ten inhalations and exhalations.*
- *Keep your eyes closed and imagine that this rope has magically been transformed into a snake—a harmless snake, but a snake nonetheless. ("That's silly," you say. Play along with me. It's just a little meditation and it may be revealing.)*
- *With your eyes still closed, reach out and touch the rope and see if you can imagine how a snake might feel as your fingers brush against its scales. Is it cold? Does it move as you touch it? Can you get just a small hint of "snakeness" in the rope? (If you have a phobia of snakes, as many people do, you may have stopped this meditation before it began. Good. Take care of yourself. You already know how powerful your projective imagination can be.)*
- *Open your eyes and consider the rope as it lies there. Let your attention turn to the possibility that there are "snakes" in your life—people or situations that you see as dangerous and harmful that may not be exactly what you project. Let your Tao Mind look at them. They may actually be snakes. They may be ropes. They most likely will be something else entirely. Who knows? What does your Tao Mind see?*

A Tao Mind Meditation

I thought I knew you
but it was only me.
The you that you truly are
is not the you I see.
My mind has formed your image
but you have already traveled on.
I want to see only you,
but I see you through me.
Forgive me.

The Magic Glasses

Acceptance sets us free.

A young woman came to the Taoist Sage to ask for help in dealing with all the things that were wrong with the world. She complained to the Sage, "I am so angry and so frustrated with the way things are. I am tired of seeing all the injustice, meanness, selfishness, greed, ignorance, and just plain wrongness that surrounds me. I want to find relief from all of that."

"Do you really want to do that?" asked the Sage. "It is a difficult practice."

"I really want to," said the woman.

The Sage considered for a moment, then reached into her tote bag and pulled out a pair of glasses. "Wear these," she told the woman. "They are enchanted glasses. When you wear them you will be able to see only those things that are acceptable to you. You will see nothing else. All of the wrong and unacceptable things will be invisible. You will see only that which pleases you."

"Wow!" exclaimed the woman. "Give me those glasses. What a relief that will be."

"Just a minute," warned the Sage. "Once you put these on, they will not come off. You will have to wear them constantly for at least a year before they can be removed. Are you willing to do that?"

"Absolutely!" cried the woman. "Give them to me!" She grabbed the glasses and put them on.

Immediately the Sage disappeared. The Sage's hut remained but most of the furniture was gone, so was the sound of the rain that had been falling on the roof. She walked out into the street and found that the marketplace was deserted. She stumbled and fell as she ran into a trash bin that had become invisible. Frantic, she tried to pull the glasses off, but found that she could not do that.

She ran to her home to talk to her husband but found that he was gone. Her next-door neighbor was gone. Everyone was gone.

"Help me," she cried. The voice of the Sage appeared from close by, startling her.

"What is it?" said the Sage.

"Everyone is gone! Everything is gone!" she wailed. "I just wanted the bad things gone, not everything."

"The glasses are revealing to you the way you actually view the world. Nothing and no one have been immune from your judgments," said the Sage. "You'll have to learn to live with the world you see."

After several weeks of stumbling in fear and confusion, the woman began to settle down and think to herself, "I miss my husband. I see how I have judged him in so many subtle ways. He is really a wonderful man."

"Hello, honey," came the familiar voice. She looked up and there stood her husband. She threw herself into his arms and sobbed.

With her husband's support she began to see the ways in which she had been insisting that people and things be what she thought they should be rather than what they actually were. Gradually more and more people began to return to her awareness, more and more things began to reappear to her sight. With each appearance came a flood of gratitude in her heart.

After a year had passed, the Sage sought her out and asked if she was ready to take the glasses off.

"Oh, yes," said the woman. "My world is rich and wonderful, but there may be things I haven't seen in a long time. I want to welcome everything back into my life— even the painful things. Even the sorrow and loss—I want to have it all. I want to know how things really are—all of it."

The Sage removed the glasses and she joyfully entered the world as it is.

* * *

I don't want to accept the world as it is. I want to accept the comfortable, joyful, and pleasant parts of it and to push away the parts I find uncomfortable, painful, and unpleasant. I want to maximize pleasure and minimize pain. Of course I do. Who doesn't?

Yet when I go about manipulating the world around me in this attempt I narrow my experience of life. I damage the things I love in my desire to eliminate the things I hate. Every time I arrange things for my own comfort I cause unintended and unanticipated consequences in my world. The comfort of my personal automobile brings unhealthy changes to my environment. The pleasure of inexpensive coffee to start my morning may mean inadequate wages for farmers in Colombia. I cannot so easily separate the world into my preferences.

I am a part of all that is and my actions affect all that is. This is not a cause for despair or immobilization. It is merely a fact of existence, and I would benefit from understanding and accepting my interdependence with all that I consider acceptable and all that I consider unacceptable. In this manner I am free to act according to my own compassionate nature without harboring the illusion that I am "perfecting" the world. I am merely being as kind and as generous as I am able. The world continues to be what it is—an inseparable dance

of life that blends acceptable and unacceptable into the necessary web of existence. Parts of me cannot accept it. Yet there is a "me," my Tao Self, that can
embrace and experience it all.

My conditioned mind loves to grab the idea of acceptance and wield it as
a heavy club above my head. "You should be more accepting," it advises. Then
it immediately points me to something so awful, so tragic that every part of
me reels back in dismay. "You can't accept that," it intones. Then it switches once
again in its never-ending game of keeping me stuck. "But you should be more
accepting."

Some sub-personalities within me will always find certain things to be
unacceptable. Other sub-personalities have a very broad tolerance of a variety
of things in the world. The Tao Mind accepts both my accepting and non-
accepting sub-personalities with affection and compassion. Neither is asked to
change.

The change and freedom we seek is found, not in forcing ourselves into being
"more forgiving," but in continually turning our attention to Tao Mind in order
to keep our perspective balanced and centered. We have parts of us who are
clinging for all they are worth to their ideas of who we should be and how we
should act. They are ready to punish and shame themselves until they "shape up,"
and it never quite works. We have other parts of us who are clinging with the

same intensity to their ideas of how other people should be and behave. They are willing to hold anger and resentment in place until these other people finally "shape up," and it never quite works either.

We have been taught that if we "accept things as they are" we are doomed to passivity and that nothing will change for the better. In fact, this is not true. Our longing for change will never be satisfied outside of our Tao Mind's generous acceptance of all that is, as it is. In the constriction of our conditioned mind and its demand for change, we find only immobilization. In the acceptance of our Tao Mind, we find room for change to flow. Remember—in forgiveness there is room for everything. In clinging, there is room for very little.

Questions for Your Tao Mind

- *Is there a particular person or situation that has long been unacceptable to you?*
- *What would it feel like if your perspective shifted and this became acceptable?*
- *Would that mean you no longer cared? Or would you be free to care in new ways?*

A Tao Mind Exercise

One of my favorite (and sometimes most uncomfortable) exercises that I do with myself and with students is called "The Acceptance Window." It is helpful to do this exercise as often as you can. You don't have to take a long time with it. Just use it to check in on how you might be identified with either an accepting or non-accepting part of yourself. Neither one is a problem. Don't try to change yourself (that would be not accepting your own non-acceptance, wouldn't it?). Just notice.

- *Draw a rectangular window on a piece of notebook paper.*
- *Lay a thin piece of wood, a ruler, or a pencil across the paper halfway down the rectangle. Above this strip write words that represent the things in life that you are able to accept right now—things that are good and fine about you and your world. Just jot down a few.*
- *Now, below the line, write several things that come to mind that are definitely "not fine" about you, other people, or the world.*
- *Now move the strip of wood down a bit and cause some of the "not fine" items to appear above the line. How does that feel?*

- *Move the strip way up to the top and make most of the items appear "below the line." How does that feel? Just notice.*
- *Now write up at the very top of the window the words "How I feel right now." Be willing to let these words always remain "above the line."*
- *Be completely honest in this exercise. You are not trying to "improve" yourself, but merely to notice, to* become aware, *of how the process of acceptance/non-acceptance operates in your life—how it affects your mood, your actions, your energy.*
- *Each time you do this exercise, the first thing you are going to consider accepting is the position of your acceptance bar. That is—"Today, I accept the feeling that my acceptance window is very narrow. Nothing feels acceptable, everything is wrong, everyone is a pain, including me." As you are willing to accept the state of your own moods and opinions, you are indicating to your self the willingness, just for a moment, to step into Tao Mind.*

A Tao Mind Meditation

I accept the judgments my conditioned mind creates.
I am more than these judgments.

I accept the many moods that come and go.

I am more than these moods.

I accept the many parts of me with tenderness and love.

I am more than these parts.

I accept my gains and losses.

I am more than these.

I accept all that is.

This I am.

My Worst Enemy

Enemies only exist in conditioned mind.

For the past ten years Jake had been in a state of almost constant torment over the way he had been treated by a business rival. "The man cheated me, slandered me, and stole from me," he would complain to anyone who would listen. "He ruined my life and he still lurks around looking for new ways to make me miserable. He is my very worst enemy!"

Jake tried everything he could think of to get rid of his enemy, short of violence. He started rumors, he complained to the Attorney General, and he considered taking the man to court but didn't want the expense of legal fees.

One day Jake was walking home from his office when he saw a strange-looking shape sitting on top of a pile of garbage in an open trash can. It seemed to be some sort of ceramic pot or vase. It was covered with dust but he could see that the workmanship was of high quality. His curiosity took over, so he lifted the vase and began to brush off some of the dirt from the top.

A powerful voice vibrated in his ear. "You have inquired of the sacred vessel. Whatever you wish will be granted to you without delay."

Jake almost dropped the vase in fright. He stood for a long moment, looking around to see if anyone was watching him or had heard the voice. No one was around.

"Well?" boomed the voice in his ear.

Something in Jake knew that this vase was truly a sacred, magic vessel. Softly he asked, "Whatever I want?"

"Whatever you want," replied the voice.

"Anything?" Jake asked.

"Anything."

Without further hesitation, Jake blurted out, "I want my worst enemy to be destroyed."

KA-POW! A bolt of lightning split the air and reduced Jake to a pile of cinders, smoldering on the ground.

• • •

People do disappoint us, betray us, harm us, even, from their perspective, hate us. This is inevitable when billions of conditioned minds interact and attempt to live as frightened, separate, and vulnerable beings. Never forget, however, that the true *enemy* always resides within the conditioned mind itself and that it is here in our conditioned mind that we can do effective work. It is here that we must deal with our enemies and here that we must find freedom.

There is a world of difference between protecting ourselves from the harmful actions of others, and wasting energy by blaming others. The Taoist warrior never considers another soldier to be an enemy to be blamed, but an opponent to be valued and honored. If even a tiny fraction of the warrior's mind is occupied with thoughts of blame toward the opponent, the battle is already lost.

I recently have been involved with an opponent of my own. For some questionable reason, the guiding board here at our Center asked me to set up an on-line system that will enable our members and students to use credit cards to pay for classes and seminars. The questionable part of this request lies not in the goal, but in the assumption that I am the person best suited for the task. But, bravely and willingly, I hitched up my Tao trousers and waded into the world of Internet commerce.

Everything went smoothly at first. "Fill out these simple online forms," I was soothingly told. "Anyone can do it." I did. We were a mere day or so away from being able to tell our members and friends, "Credit cards accepted." Then an e-mail appeared in my in-box informing me that our "account had been frozen pending further investigation."

What! Account frozen. What account? What do you mean by "frozen"? It sounds like something done to a cancerous mole before cutting it off. Well, it turns out that this is bank-speak for requesting a bit more information—supporting documents and such. Talk about frozen—every part of my conditioned mind freezes up when confronted with the world of "supporting documents." What documents? What if I send the wrong ones? Will I go to jail?

Fortunately I am part of a community that supports me in the practice of seeing everything in my experience as an opportunity for awareness and freedom. Instead of having my colleagues say, "No problem, we'll take over and handle it for you," I was told, "What a great chance to see deeper into your conditioning. You can do it." And I could.

A decades-old conditioned process in me is that of "that which I need will be withheld from me because I am not good enough." A corollary to that process is "and those who are in the position to do the withholding are my enemies."

I had two choices for viewing the work, because I was going to do it in either case. The first choice was to view whoever "they" were on the bank side of this task as my enemies who were eager to withhold from me and punish me for my inadequacies. Or I could view them as ordinary people whose true nature is more than happy to help, if given the chance. I chose the second option.

Phone conversations took on a new tone. "Help me, please," I said. "We will," they replied. They did. The whole process became just part of the "stuff" of my life that helps me see how I separate myself from myself, and create my enemies within. When I can see it, I can change it. And I do.

My conditioned mind warns me, "There are real enemies out there and you'd better darn well believe it. There are terrorists and other crazies who would delight in killing you."

Isn't it interesting the way certain internal voices get so agitated at the mere mention that we may not need to have the conflict-ridden life that seems to be our lot? It is as if the mere entertaining of the thought of forgiving enemies will be tantamount to painting a sign on my door, "Ax Murderers Welcome."

Of course there are people and situations that are truly dangerous. Tao Mind would not suggest otherwise. But these people and situations are far rarer than my conditioning would have me believe, *and* my safety lies, not in creating a category of "enemy" to contain these things, but in letting my Tao Mind bring forgiveness to *all* the categories I have created in an effort to protect myself. My

Tao Mind does not see life in terms of these categories. It allows me to forgive myself and others whenever my conditioned mind seeks to impose new categories on situations and people. Forgiveness removes the separation that categories such as "enemies" create, freeing us to see clearly and act with our inherent compassion.

Questions for Your Tao Mind

- *Does not seeing people as "enemies" make us more at risk?*
- *Is there such a thing as a true "enemy"?*
- *Can even true "enemies" be forgiven?*

A Tao Mind Exercise

I call this my "Richard Nixon" exercise.

- *Sit with your journal and turn your attention to your breath.*
- *Write at the top of a new page the title: "Enemies List."*

- *Spend some time with this list. You don't have to censor it or try to be good and "Tao-like" in making it. You are letting your fearful sub-personalities have the floor and communicate honestly all of the people and circumstances that they feel are likely to cause them some kind of harm.*
- *List people from childhood, school, work, family, society, other cultures, groups, organizations, nations—anyone or any group that some part of you sees, or has seen in the past, as having the potential to cause you harm.*
- *After you have come to a stopping place in your "enemies" list, make another list. Title this one: "How I handle these enemies."*
- *For each "enemy" make a note of what effect this person or group has on your life. The effect could be as large as a direct and immediate threat or as small as a nagging worry in the back of your mind.*
- *Note also the actions you take with regard to this person or group. How much time and energy is used?*
- *When you finish, stand up and stretch. Walk around for a bit and turn your attention to the sensations in your arms and legs.*
- *Sit down and pick one item from your list. Write for a bit on the question: "If this person (or group) were in my life for my benefit, what would be different about my experience?"*
- *What particular enemy, or simple "pain in the neck," in your life could you*

use to practice bringing your attention to this premise? Don't try to get your conditioned mind to agree. Just give some consideration to how the Tao Mind might use your experience to help you see through your clinging, resentment, fear, etc.

A Tao Mind Meditation

Conflict does not separate me from myself.
It shows me how I have learned to be afraid.
It teaches me a different way to be
and returns me to my Tao Mind
where I find my enemies
have become my honored teachers.

Right or Wrong?

Mistakes are not wrong.

Once a Taoist Master served as an elementary school teacher. His classroom felt much like an ordinary classroom. Any difference you might notice was subtle but might be seen in the way the Master invited children to answer questions. For instance, one day he asked for a student to work a mathematics problem on the board.

Jimmy eagerly raised his hand, stretching it as far as he could reach toward the ceiling. "Teacher, teacher, I know. I know. Call on me, please, teacher."

Carol slid down in her seat wishing she had a Harry Potter wand and could cast an invisibility spell. "Please, oh please," she thought, "please don't call on me."

The teacher walked up to Carol and handed her the chalk. "Carol, go up and give it a try. I'll help you figure it out."

"Oh, God," thought Carol, not moving, "I don't know. I can't."

"It's scary, isn't it?!" said the teacher in a tender, encouraging voice. "Please try. It doesn't matter if you do it right or not."

Carol croaked a faint reply, "I c-c-can't do it."

"Then," said the teacher, "there are probably lots of other students who can't do it either. Let's go up to the board and figure it out."

Carol slowly rose and walked the long mile up to the board. She took the chalk in her hand and tried to see the numbers on the board through her emerging tears. She took a deep breath and wrote down what she could remember of the solution, but she really didn't understand what she was doing.

"You're right on track with the first part," said the teacher. "Let me see the chalk." She took the chalk from Carol and wrote other numbers in place of some that Carol had written. "Does that look correct?" she asked Carol. Carol looked for a long minute and suddenly saw what the teacher had done and why she wrote those particular numbers.

"Yes!" she said. "Yes, that really is right. That's how it's done!" She was beaming.

Turning to the class, the teacher said, "It is not hard at all to write on the board when you know the answer. Serious students are the ones willing and brave enough to stand up at the board when they don't know how to do it."

Carol returned to her seat feeling a great sense of relief and freedom.

• • •

Most teachers are dedicated, loving, and sincere in their desire to educate children. Yet from a child's perspective, Carol's experience is not always what happens. Without conscious intention or cruelty, all parts of our society tend, from the moment we are born, to reward us for being right and punish us for being wrong. Our conditioned mind quickly learns that being right is more pleasing to other people than being wrong. In fact, being wrong is downright dangerous. It brings frowns from adults and laughter from our peers. A very un-Taoist approach by a teacher might unfold something like this:

"Carol," intoned the teacher from behind her massive desk, "please come to the board and do this problem for us."

"Oh, God," thought Carol, not moving, "I don't know. I can't."

"Carol!" said the teacher in the no-nonsense, you're-on-the-verge-of-trouble voice. "Please come to the board."

Carol croaked a faint reply, "I c-c-can't do it."

"What?" said the teacher. "Speak up, young lady. We can't hear you."

"I-I-I don't know how to do it," Carol said.

"You get up to the board, young lady. Let's see what you know."

Carol slowly rose and walked the long mile up to the board. She took the chalk in her hand and tried to see the numbers on the board through her emerging tears. She took a deep breath and wrote down what she could remember of the solution, but she really didn't understand what she was doing.

"That's wrong," said the teacher. "I assumed as much. Sit down." Turning to the class, she asked, "Does anyone know how to do the problem right? Jimmy, why don't you come up and do it for us."

Jimmy eagerly dashed to the board and, in large bold characters, quickly wrote out the solution to the problem.

"Very good." The teacher smiled. "Very good, Jimmy. Now, let's go on to the next problem."

Carol cried softly to herself, much to the amusement of those around her.

We may or may not have experienced similar situations in our school years, but I would guess that all of us are familiar with internal dialogues that evoke the same emotions—"I must do this right. I don't know how. I'm in trouble."

In the first story Carol was invited to make a mistake and rewarded for her willingness to learn from it. In the second she was shamed for being wrong. Isn't that an interesting combination of words?—"being wrong." "Being" implies that the wrongness is something inherent in my existence, not just in my knowledge. I didn't just say or do something that was mistaken; I *am* wrong.

Tao Mind forgiveness is rooted in the realization that there is nothing wrong with being wrong. My Tao Mind is eager to make mistakes, because making mistakes means that there is something I don't currently know that I have the opportunity to learn. My Tao Mind would love a school in which a room full of children eagerly stretch their hands toward the ceiling crying, "Oh, teacher, I don't know that one. Let me learn!" These children would be following in the footsteps of Thomas Edison, whose greatest achievement lay in the thousands of times he was "wrong" before he found a consistent model for the electric lightbulb.

But the conditioned mind remains terrified of being wrong. Because of that terror, our mind constructs a scrutinizing system that constantly monitors our behavior and the behavior of others to ascertain whether it is "right" or "wrong." Bless our mind—it is truly trying to keep us safe and help us maneuver through the tricky shoals of society. It is not bad for doing so. It has just created patterns that do not necessarily serve us as we seek the freedom of forgiveness.

When a youngster such as Carol becomes terrified of not knowing, of being wrong, a sub-personality emerges that sees itself through that filter. This part of us does not see itself as merely mistaken, or not knowing. The subtle, or not-so-subtle, message that is heard is: "You don't know because there is something wrong with you—you are flawed!"

Our conditioned sub-personalities are longing to hear someone call them "willing and brave," but they seldom experience such words. Instead they hear habitual mental patterns repeat the refrain: "There is something wrong with you and you'd better either fix it or hide it." With such mental habits becoming the dominant internal voices over the decades, is it any wonder that forgiveness is a problem? Is it any wonder that forgiveness becomes one more thing that we are "not doing right"? "You might be forgiven," our conditioned mind will concede, "but we all know that there is still something wrong with you." That "something wrong" will not go away no matter how many words of forgiveness are spoken.

But if there is nothing inherently wrong with me, it is possible that the harm I have done and the harm I have experienced in my life is due to fear and ignorance. This means that freedom and forgiveness are true possibilities. I can face my fears and understand them—I am capable of that. I can learn that which I do not know—I am capable of that. My heart can be broken, because at its very core, it is good and that very goodness is the reason it can recover from its brokenness. Other people can have their hearts broken and recover as well.

We may be afraid and mistaken, but our true nature is Tao Mind and the freedom to make any mistake and be forgiven is always available.

Questions for Your Tao Mind

- *Do you remember some ways in which you were taught the danger of "being wrong"?*
- *Do you remember a time when you discovered the value inherent in "being wrong"?*
- *Are there memories of "being wrong" that need to be brought to your Tao Mind and released into forgiveness?*

A Tao Mind Exercise—A Drama

- *Let's create a short, improvisational play in our imagination. You will be taking all of the roles in this play, so let your inner actor have the stage for a bit.*

- *Cast: (You supply the names.)*
  - *Young child, around six or seven years old*
  - *Older child, nine or ten years old*
  - *Adult authority figure*
  - *Adult representing Tao Mind*
- *The young child is in a situation where she/he feels out of place and frightened and is asked to do something she/he doesn't know how to do. The older child knows how to do this and is impatient with and irritated at the younger child. The adult authority figure wants the younger child to shape up and do it right so he/she can get on with the day. The Tao Mind adult is deeply tender toward all of the other characters, does not see any of them as "wrong," and interacts with each of them in an open, accepting, and encouraging manner.*
- *Take your time with this exercise. This is Method Acting—let yourself sink into each character and become that character. You may want to find a place where you can actually set up the stage and act it out. (Don't do this in a coffee shop or office. There is nothing wrong with that, but let's not push it.) You may want to write out the script. If you get blocked on a particular character, try writing that character's dialogue with your nondominant hand.*
- *Save the Tao Mind adult until you have a good sense of the feelings and*

reactions of the other characters. Then let the Tao Mind interact with each in turn. Tao Mind does not have the agenda to "solve" anything. It merely listens, talks, accepts, encourages, and loves. In the same way, you are not trying to solve or fix anything with this exercise. You are gently letting yourself become aware of and find a bit more openness to the parts of you that are involved in the shame and blame habits that keep forgiveness from being a present-moment reality in your life.

• Be especially aware of the sensations and feelings you have when you are "in" each role. If you get stuck, take a break and come back to the drama later in the evening or the next day when you have a bit of time. Be curious. Have fun. No one is watching for you to do this right. (Or is there someone, even as you read these words, who really does expect you to do this exercise in some "correct" way? Isn't that interesting? You may want to create a drama involving that particular character someday.)

A Tao Mind Meditation

There is nothing wrong with me.
There is nothing wrong with those inside my head

or in my outer life, who think
that there is something wrong with me.
We are all doing the best we know how.
We all belong to the Tao.
We can be tender.
We can be free.

Zebras and Lions

Fear does not bring safety.

Two zebras, Bob and Ted, were part of a large herd that spent its days grazing happily across the African savanna. Grass grew with abundance because the rains had been timely this past year but Bob was complaining to Ted, "You know, there might not be enough grass next year. You never can tell. It doesn't seem fair that we have to depend on something as unreliable as the weather in order to have enough to eat."

Ted murmured an acknowledgment while continuing to munch and enjoy the grass. Bob went on, "And the lions! It wouldn't be so bad if it weren't for the lions. You never know when they are going to show up, hungry and eager to kill us. It's just wrong. They shouldn't do that. Something should be done about it. Who do they think they are?"

"They're lions," said his friend. "That's what they do."

"I don't care," said Bob. "It's just not right. We have to be constantly on our guard, never relaxing, never safe."

"I'm relaxed," said Ted, "and there are no hungry lions around."

"Hmph," snorted Bob, and he went back to eating. But he seldom enjoyed even the most succulent of grasses because his stomach tended to be tight most of the time.

Later that afternoon as the herd was relaxing in the shade and Bob was complaining about the way wildebeests hogged the water, Ted suddenly bolted and ran. "Lions!" he shouted over his shoulder. Bob was so distracted by his complaints that he was two steps slower than Ted. He was also tense and his muscles didn't respond easily and smoothly, causing him to lose another two steps.

Four steps were all the lions needed.

The lion is predator and the zebra is prey. But it is not the zebra's fear that serves to help it escape the lion—it is its innate intelligence and ability to react instantly, without second thoughts. The zebra does not blame the lion for being a lion. In a sense, the zebra "forgives" the lion. When the lion walks by a zebra herd and is not hunting, the zebras hardly glance up. They notice the lion and go back to munching grass. If, however, the lion is in a hunting mood, the zebra herd knows immediately and every member of the herd becomes alert. Still, they continue to go about their business of grazing. When the lion attacks, the zebras react instantly. Often the zebra is too quick and the lion remains hungry. Occasionally an older, sickly, or otherwise vulnerable zebra will fall to the lions. This is the way of the Tao.

It is also the way of the Tao that each individual is equipped with instinctive qualities that allow it to be completely capable of its life—capable of nourishing itself, caring for itself, responding to danger—AND—capable of illness, accident, old age, and death. The animal that remains centered on these natural qualities lives a life of intense awareness and wonder. The animal that distracts itself from these qualities diminishes the awareness and the wonder, lives a narrower and more fearful life; it clings to resentment and anger, and makes itself more vulnerable to the very things it hates and fears.

Forgiveness is necessary to keep our fears from freezing us in a "something's wrong" mind. It is the quality of our Tao Mind that allows us to return to our natural capabilities. When conditioned mind grabs hold of guilt or resentment and clings to it, our attention is removed from the present moment. We find ourselves seeing all the things that are wrong with life in general and with our life in particular. "Something's wrong" robs life of its intrinsic joys and pleasures while doing nothing to more effectively help us face the challenges of life.

We all have the equivalent of "lions" in our life—those people who do not behave as we think they should; people whose behavior we feel is a threat to our safety. How do we best prepare ourselves for lions? By learning to pay relaxed, yet alert, attention to the "what is" of our life in the present moment, and to forgive whatever lions may be part of our life. That way, when the present moment offers actual lions, we will be able to take whatever action is necessary without being slowed by a burden of resentment. In the meantime, we are experiencing the full measure of our life in all of its tastes, smells, sights, tasks, joys, disappointments, and wonders. When we turn our attention to our Tao Mind, we are essentially forgiving life for being what it is—forgiving it for containing the lions of sickness, death, loss, and sorrow. The same space that accepts these lions of life also contains our gratitude for health, love, wonder, and joy. We don't get just part of life, we get it all.

There is nothing wrong with me for being afraid. I have been consistently schooled in the economics and politics of fear, and I don't need to punish myself for having learned my lesson well. But I really don't want to be the zebra who spends his life missing the taste of grass and the warmth of the sun because of his fearful "something wrong mind," and then ends up unaware when action is actually required in the present moment.

Most lions in my life are not really lions but merely "ideas of lions" presented by various forms of media. Trying to make room for my Tao Mind, I limit my exposure to media. The very nature of the word "media" implies a mediated experience of life, and I prefer my experience to be direct. But certain words and images that pass themselves off as "information" manage to be collected by my conditioned mind anyway. As I write these words the world seems to be facing a long list of fears. News of terrorism, financial meltdown, global warming leading to a new ice age, toxic waste, and wars of all varieties fill the screens and pages of our mediated lives.

Yet at this particular moment, I am sitting with a hot cup of coffee, writing these words and looking out the café window on a dim, wet December morning. In a few moments I will join members of my community for our regular morning meditation. Then I will fix breakfast and probably return to this manuscript.

My conditioned mind, however, has seized upon a headline it managed to sneak by my guard, a headline that screamed of the latest disastrous financial news. I am now being told by an authoritative inner voice that (1) this book is a waste of time, (2) I should be out looking for a *real* job, and (3) I will probably end my days huddled homeless under a bridge. Useful information? Utter garbage, designed to keep me running from imaginary lions until I am too exhausted to do the actual work of my life, which, at this moment, is to be writing this book, here in this café, on this invigorating morning.

"Forgive, forgive, forgive," I whisper to myself in rhythm with my breath. I release these numerous ideas and conditioned fears. Life does contain real lions and I must forgive it for that. I would rather there were no threats to my safety and well-being, but only forgiveness will allow enough space in my experience to see them when they actually appear and to take appropriate action in the moment. In the meantime, there is a cup of hot coffee.

Questions for Your Tao Mind

- *What "lions" are in your mind right now?*
- *Can you forgive them for being whatever or whoever they are?*
- *Are they real lions, or merely the "idea of lions"? You can usually tell by asking if there is any specific action that is needed in the present moment. If not, let the fear soften and turn your attention to what is actually before you.*

A Tao Mind Exercise

- *Select a daily newspaper that contains articles on national, international, and financial news.*
- *Sit in a meditative position on your cushion or on a comfortable chair. Have your notebook/journal at hand.*
- *Read every article in the national, international, and financial sections.*
- *As you read each article, ask yourself:*
- *"Who"—what sub-personality within you—is reading?*
    What is this part of you being told about what you are reading?
    What sensations do you notice in your body?
    What are you being told this article "means" about your life?
    What are you being told you "should" be doing?
    Who and what needs to be brought into the spacious forgiveness of your Tao Mind in order for you to be free and present with your life?
- *After reading each article and answering the above, stand, stretch, and take several deep breaths and let your attention turn to your Tao Mind, to a feeling of spacious awareness. Then go on to the next article.*

- *When you are finished with the paper, notice any overall effects on your bodily sensations and state of mind. Is there any urgency in your mind? If so, let this urgency settle back into spacious awareness and let yourself become aware of all of the sights, smells, sounds, and textures of your surroundings.*
- *Bring remaining tensions and urgencies into your Tao Mind and see if you can make space for them to dissipate.*

Tao Mind Meditation

*We are here to bring forgiveness
to ourselves and to the world.
We are not here to be afraid
or to cling to the anxiety
that separates us from life.
We are here to use everything in our experience
to see how we cling and suffer,
so we can gently set it down,
and find forgiveness for ourselves
and for the world.*

Master Dave's Coat

Rules do not bring freedom.

The monastery was located in the foothills just outside a small Oregon coastal town. It was a relatively new monastery, only fifteen years old, but the strong leadership of Master Dave had attracted a following of fifteen dedicated monks, both men and women, who worked diligently building simple hermitages for people on retreat, maintaining the gardens, cooking, cleaning, meditating, and keeping the strict rules of monastic life.

One young monk, however, was ambivalent. Part of him wanted to find peace and freedom through the rigorous discipline of the monastery. Another part of him missed the pleasures of society. He devised a strategy by which he hoped he could satisfy both parts. Several evenings each week he would wait until everyone was asleep and then sneak out of his hermitage, quietly open the gate, and walk the two miles into town where he would enjoy an hour or two of food, drink, music, and the company of women. He would sneak back to his hermitage in the early morning hours and try to sleep for a few hours before the morning bell.

He wasn't as clever as he thought. The other monks found out that he was breaking the rules and, one by one, they went to Master Dave and complained. "He has made a mockery of our monastery," they said. "You have to get rid of him." Master Dave nodded and said quietly, "I'll take care of it."

The next time the monk silently opened the gate and sneaked through it, he found Master Dave sitting on a stump waiting for him with a heavy coat draped across his lap. Master Dave smiled and handed him the coat, saying, "It is cold tonight and a long walk into town. Here, wear my coat. You can hang it on the hook outside my door when you return." With that, Master Dave bowed to the young monk and went back inside.

The young monk was astonished and embarrassed. He didn't know what to do. Finally he put on the warm coat and walked slowly into town. He remained at the corner bar only a short while, lost in thought, oblivious to the music and company. He walked back to the monastery, hung up Master Dave's coat, and went to the meditation hall.

The next morning as the monks filed into the hall, they found the young monk *still there, deep in meditation. Later in the day each of the other monks came to Master Dave and voiced their outrage. "You said you would get rid of him," they said.*

"I said I would take care of it," Master Dave replied, "and I did."

"You mean he's going to stay!" they said in astonishment.

"Of course he is going to stay. He wants to find freedom. Where else can he go?" replied Master Dave.

"What if he continues to break the rules and sneak out?"

"Then I'll continue to lend him my coat," said Master Dave.

The monks were angry and frustrated. This was unacceptable. They wanted rules to be taken seriously. By the end of that day, fourteen of them had packed their belongings and left. They each traveled in search of a monastery where rules would be enforced. As they traveled they spread the story of the horrible state of the discipline at Master Dave's monastery. Only Master Dave and the young wayward monk remained.

"What shall we do?" the young monk asked.

"Tend the garden, cook our meals, clean up, chop our wood, and meditate," said Master Dave.

Together they worked in meditative silence from morning until night, tending the garden, cooking their meals, cleaning up, chopping wood, and meditating. By the time the young monk returned to his hermitage in the evening he was too tired to even consider the walk into town. He was concerned. He knew that the two of them could not keep the monastery open for long. But each morning he awoke eager to spend the day in work.

A week passed. One Wednesday afternoon a young woman arrived at the gate. She said that she had heard the story of Master Dave's coat. She asked if she could be a part of a monastery where "forgiveness was the rule." Master Dave welcomed her. Several days later two older men arrived. They had traveled over a thousand miles after hearing about Master Dave's coat and asked if they could please stay. By the end of six months the monastery housed thirty monks.

The monastery thrived. Many people came to enjoy times of retreat in the company of this joyful group of monks. New buildings were built. New gardens were planted. The rules remained—silence, work, discipline, schedules, rituals, and the like. The rules were seldom broken. When they were, the monks all smiled to themselves and thought of Master Dave's coat, still hanging outside his door, a constant reminder of the forgiveness waiting in a compassionate heart.

My spouse and I try to spend some time each year at the monastery that is our own place of training. It is located in the foothills near Angel's Camp, California, about four hours from our home. When we are there we live as monks—in silence and in separate hermitages. We work, meditate, and sometimes have guided discussions with our own teacher. There are many guidelines at our monastery—silence, no reading, no phones, no computers, a certain way of preparing food, cleaning up, entering the hall, leaving our shoes in certain places, and so on.

We all forget the guidelines from time to time—because we are distracted, busy, or just because we are tired of the "silly rules." When we do, we receive a polite note saying, "Please remember . . ." Breaking what some people would call "rules" is an essential part of our practice. Noticing how we feel when we break them, how we treat ourselves afterward, how we respond to being reminded— all these are opportunities for awareness and are essential to our growing freedom.

There is a sign prominently displayed in the dining hall. It states:

"We have many guidelines, but only one rule: We will use everything in our experience to see how we cause ourselves to suffer, so we can drop that, and end suffering."

Rules, whether they are internal or external, are dangerous tools. On the one hand, they provide a certain stability for our societies and for our personal experience. On the other hand, they easily become ends in themselves—slave masters whose purpose is to keep us in bondage rather than lead us to freedom. They become devices for punishment, supplying the ammunition used by parts of our conditioned mind to keep up a continuous barrage of accusations of "wrongness" directed at ourselves and at others.

If, instead, we look to compassionate guidelines for our support, we find gentle tools that reveal to us how we resist, divert, distract, repress, and avoid the direct experience of our life. Guidelines become the things we "bump against" that keep us awake. In order for guidelines to function in this manner, forgiveness must be a constant presence in our heart. Without forgiveness, rules, no matter how trivial, become cruel whips wielded by our conditioned mind to keep us in line.

I am experiencing the subtle nudge of rules/guidelines at this very moment. I am writing at home on a cold, gray, rain-soaked afternoon. It is the day before Christmas and I just arrived home from a trip to the library to return some books. The traffic was insane, even in our modest-sized California valley town. I am a bit cold and uncomfortable. I have to go out again later for meditation at our Center. *I don't want to sit down and write!* Yet my guideline, established in cooperation with my spouse and others in my community, tells me that the next two hours are to be set aside for writing.

I am alone. No one is enforcing this guideline. I want, *really want,* to open a bag of chips, pour a soft drink, and sit down with my feet up, read a book, and feel a bit sorry for myself, indulging that part of my conditioning that dislikes this season. Maybe a few pieces of chocolate candy and a *big* bag of chips—no one would know.

As you can tell, I am writing in spite of my urges. If, instead, I stop and choose the chips and candy route, I would not be a bad person. I would not punish myself. Whatever choice I make, I get to see the conditioned processes that are so deeply ingrained in my life.

When we so continuously see the world through the lenses of rules, we are set up for disappointment, resentment, guilt, and shame. No one keeps the rules. No one even knows all the rules because they constantly change and multiply. We have all read different "Rule Books" and get frightened when others ignore "our" rules. Only the forgiveness residing in the compassionate conscious awareness of our Tao Mind can ever free us from the trap we are in.

I need and benefit from guidelines. Without them I would be stuffing chips into my mouth and reading trashy science fiction right now. Yet I cannot allow them to become agents of conditioned self-hate, self-punishment, and resentment toward others. Knowing that forgiveness rather than punishment awaits in my Tao Mind allows me to have a growth-oriented relationship to the rules and guidelines of my life. I am able to commit to certain guidelines, not as a slave dominated by fear of punishment, but as a free and willing person. Forgiveness frees me to use the guidelines to help me pay attention to the way my conditioned mind attempts to keep me unconscious of the habitual thoughts and actions that tend to dominate my life. Guidelines, coupled with forgiveness, bring freedom.

Questions for Your Tao Mind

- *Are there some rules that seem absolute, the breaking of which is so awful that forgiveness doesn't seem possible? How might you compassionately support yourself as you work with these rules?*
- *Does practicing forgiveness with the "small" rules help you when you face the more serious transgressions in yourself or others?*
- *Can you use "rule-breaking" as an opportunity to bring more compassionate attention to yourself and others?*

A Tao Mind Exercise

- *Sit in a comfortable position with your pen and notebook.*
- *At the top of a blank page write: "Rules."*

• *Begin noticing and writing down some of the rules by which you live and by which you expect others to live. List about ten.*
• *Consider each rule with the following in mind:*

  Is this a rule or a guideline?

  What happens when I break this rule?

  What do I tell myself it means about me when I break this rule?

  What do I tell myself about others when they break this rule?

  Are there different voices in my conditioned mind that each have a different perspective on the "breaking of the rule"?

  What might your Tao Mind tell you when you or others break this rule?

A Tao Mind Meditation

People should behave.
They should be brave, clean, reverent, thrifty, and kind.
They should do their chores,
mind their mothers,
and never talk too loud.
When they don't behave

I am afraid.
Who and what can I count on
if rules are not rules?
I can count on the courage of my own heart,
the compassion of my own nature,
and the forgiveness always waiting in my Tao Mind.

I'm Not Thinking About You

Each person is capable of life.

Bob was head over heels in love with Connie. His whole life was consumed with the wonder, the beauty, the warmth, and the joy of having her in his life. She seemed to return his love and he spent long hours dreaming about the exciting and fulfilling future they would create together.

Bob's mind was constantly filled with thoughts of her. He felt anxious when he was apart from her and could barely concentrate on his work. When they were together again, he would relax and reassure himself that "everything's all right. She loves me. I'm okay."

As time passed, Bob began to sense that Connie was changing. He began to worry that he was losing her love, so he constantly asked her for reassurance. "Do you really love me?" he would ask twenty times a day. Connie would be evasive in her reply and Bob's anxiety increased as he felt she was having second thoughts. In fact, Connie was becoming uncomfortable with being the object of the kind of obsessive love Bob seemed to be displaying.

Things got worse and worse and Bob became more and more frantic. Finally Connie told him in clear words that, though she had thought she might love him and want to be with him, she no longer felt that way. She sadly said that she wanted to stop seeing him and that she wanted to go on with her life without him.

Bob was panicked and depressed. He tried to honor her request but couldn't stop himself from calling and writing her, trying to convince her to change her mind. She became angry as his obsession continued and told him in strong words to back off.

He tried to forget her but his mind remained filled with memories of being with her. He could not imagine how she could just stop loving him. He needed her. He couldn't imagine himself living without her. Months went by and Bob managed not to bother Connie, but his sadness, grief, and disappointment remained. He also had flashes of anger. "How could she do this to me?" Whether it was anger or grief, she continued to fill both his waking moments and his dreams.

One day, he accidentally came across her in the grocery store. His heart pounded as he tried to speak to her. He began to tell her how much he missed her and how he thought about her constantly. She stopped him. She looked directly at him and said with a firm yet kind voice, "Bob, you need to understand—all the time that you are thinking about me, I'm not thinking of you. Do you understand? I'm not thinking about you." She put her hand on his shoulder and said a final time, "I'm sorry it hurts you, but I'm not thinking about you at all." She turned and walked away.

Bob remained rooted to the place, but his mind reeled. He turned and slowly walked away, his heart finally broken, his life over. "She doesn't think of me at all." Strangely, however, by the time he reached home his step felt just a bit lighter. He poured himself a soft drink and sat down on his porch. "She isn't thinking of me," he mused, "yet I am consumed with thoughts of her. Hmm."

The next morning he awoke and, for a few moments, forgot that he was miserable. He fixed coffee and went again to his chair on the front porch. Suddenly he remembered to remember her, but quickly the thought "She's not thinking of me" created a space in his mind. He began to notice the colors of the autumn leaves, just beginning to turn, along the tree-lined street. He remembered that he would be attending an interesting presentation at the office that morning. He began to muse about a few ideas that might make the office computer systems work a bit more effectively. He smiled, got up, and went inside to prepare some eggs for breakfast.

• • •

There are three important truths to remember in the practice of forgiveness:

1. Every person is capable of his/her own life.
2. You are capable of your own life.
3. Forgiveness allows this basic capability to emerge.

We, of course, live in community with one another and depend upon one another in many ways. Our Tao Mind naturally responds in compassion to others when our conditioned mind steps aside. But part of that compassionate response rests on the knowledge that the other person is capable of whatever comes. Tao Mind cares for other people but never usurps authority for their lives.

Connie's response to Bob that day in the grocery store may have been straight from the compassionate awareness of her Tao Mind. In any case, it gave Bob the jolt he needed to break the obsessive pattern his conditioning had set up. His Tao Mind became free to turn its compassion to his own wounds and feelings. His attention was freed from its prison of "what should be" and was now able to see "what is." He will have many more times of sadness and loss as his conditioned memories rise to the surface. But they will gradually lose their ability to make him miserable. He will be able to turn his attention back to the direct experience of his life. His conditioning will no longer be focused on "missing her," and therefore he will not miss his own life as it unfolds. He will forgive her and move on.

Our conditioned mind can easily label people who do not think about us in the way we desire as selfish, cold, or unfeeling. This labeling occurs because we naturally want to be supported and loved by our human community. The real suffering comes from our inability to trust that such support and love is, in truth, flowing constantly into, through, and out from our Tao Mind. Because we don't often experience this basic trust in life, we cling to our labels and judgments of other people. We are unable to forgive because we don't trust our own capabilities or the capabilities of others.

One of my most active sub-personalities is the one I would label the "nice" boy.

"You're such a *nice* boy, Billy," was the endlessly repeated refrain from my childhood. "You're not like those other boys who are loud, rude, aggressive, and [horrors!] *not nice.*"

Nice, of course, meant smiling, accommodating, quiet, obedient, and helpful to his parents and other adults. Nice behavior brought the rewards of smiles, praise, and privileges. All behavior that was "not nice" was frightening and unthinkable to this little one who wanted so much to be accepted.

Being this nice was difficult because it meant discerning what each person in my outer life wanted and then adjusting my persona to comply with that want. It caused me to develop a super-sensitive radar system for scoping out what other people expected, what would make them feel good and reward me with the oh-so-important words of praise. And since I worked so hard at this task, I certainly expected other people to be nice as well. We should all be . . . well . . . nice. You can imagine how much pain and suffering this sub-personality has been through in sixty years of trying to be nice and make others nice in return.

Compassion is not always nice. Words that truly arise from compassion, forgiveness, and freedom are often not at all the words that our sub-personalities want to hear. I've done quite a bit of harm in my life in my attempts to stay safe by being nice. When I was in my early twenties I caused, I think, a great deal of pain in one intimate relationship when I didn't have the courage to say, "I'm not thinking about you." I kept being "nice" and allowed another person to remain unable to go on with her life.

"Are you saying that we *shouldn't* think about the feelings of other people, that we *shouldn't* be nice?"

It has been my experience that our Tao Mind, in its spacious compassion, deeply cares about the well-being of all other beings and would never deliberately cause harm to anyone. Because the Tao Mind sees with clarity, it is able to speak with clarity. This clarity always arises from a well of compassion and of course tries to frame its communication in kind and helpful terms. It doesn't have to *act* nice, because it *is* nice.

When we disappoint other people or they disappoint us, we have the opportunity to use Tao Mind forgiveness to create a space for us to speak and act with clear compassion. We don't have to be trapped in either "being nice" or "being cruel." Since both we and the other person are fundamentally capable of finding forgiveness, we can risk speaking truthfully. If either our words or theirs cause harm, we have the practice of forgiveness to support us and keep us willing to continue to learn to speak and act with clarity, compassion, and truth.

Questions for Your Tao Mind

- *In trying to be clear, is an ego sub-personality subtly trying to get needs met rather than speaking with compassion and truth?*
- *Do I actually even know what would be "best" for another person?*
- *Can I trust other people to be capable for their life, even if my words cause pain?*
- *Can I trust myself to be capable for my life, even if others deeply wound me?*

A Tao Mind Exercise

- *Sit with your journal and let your attention come to be with your breath.*
- *Write down and consider these questions: What have I learned about "being nice" and how has this conditioning been of benefit? How has it been harmful?*
- *As you consider the questions, notice if you can identify a particular sub-personality whose job is to "be nice."*
- *Is there a sub-personality who reacts to the "nice one" by resisting, rebelling, and lashing out, sometimes causing the very harm you seek to avoid? (This is a common reaction to the attempts of our conditioned mind to control things.)*
- *What would your Tao Mind say to each of the sub-personalities involved in the "niceness" process? Remember that the Tao Mind is not interested in changing any of these parts of you, only in accepting, understanding, and seeing the fear that lies beneath their conditioning.*

A Tao Mind Meditation

May all those whom I have harmed,
deliberately or accidentally,
be free from thought about it.
May they not miss a moment of their life
through thoughts about my failures.
May I be free from thought
about the harm others have done to me,
deliberately or accidentally.
May I not miss a moment of my life.

The Nightmare

Separateness is a dream.

No unhappiness ever seemed to touch the village of Wu, situated on the bank of the river Wei. The villagers of Wu were content to live their lives in harmony with whatever direction the Tao would take. They could have prosperity and health or famine and sickness and never lose their serenity because they each knew they were expressions of the Tao and forever at home in the Tao.

One night a young girl named Maya experienced a most horrible nightmare. In her dream all of the people in the village had been transformed into monsters. They still looked like her friends and family, but inside they were possessed by evil spirits. In her dream she was all alone, the only person unaffected by these evil spirits. She could no longer trust anybody and had to be on her guard at every moment. It was *a terrifying dream. This horrible dream was so vivid that when she awoke she continued to believe that these terrible things were real.*

In her waking life she began to lash out at her family and friends. She was convinced that they were evil inside and would try to harm her if they could, so she did whatever she could to protect herself. She began to steal valuables from them so she would have the things she felt she needed to be safe. The villagers came to her and told her she must stop stealing. They tried to show her that she was safe and loved and did not need to fear. She fought them with viciousness and fury, leaving one older man severely wounded.

Finally they were able to subdue her and put her under guard in a village elder's house. Each day people from the village would visit her, bringing food and gifts. Each day she would accept their gifts but she remained suspicious and hostile. Each day they would talk to her of their love, and each day she would reject them in her fear. Three years later she still believed her dream was real and still remained under guard. Each day she was fed and cared for with loving kindness.

One day a visitor to the village saw how kindly she was being treated and said to the village leader in astonishment, "You are wasting valuable resources on this woman. She has done harm to the village, yet you treat her with special kindness. She should be punished, beaten, and taught a lesson. She should not be rewarded for her crimes."

"Punished?" said the leader. "Do you punish your child for having a nightmare? She is dreaming. We care for her in the hopes that she may one day wake up."

Why were the villagers so willing and so capable of forgiving Maya? Because they knew her nightmare was just a dream. They could take whatever steps were necessary to keep themselves from being harmed by Maya's delusion. They could even keep her captive when her actions became too dangerous. But they could also continue to love, forgive, and work with her because they knew she was believing an illusion, a dream. How can you punish someone who believes their dreams are real?

For forgiveness to truly settle into our experience, we must be in the process of waking up from our terrible dream—a dream that has seemed so real for so long that to question it is to seem to question the very foundations of our being.

We are all Maya. We all believe that our dream of being only a separate, isolated self is real. Believing that dream, we naturally act from fear and self-protection. We protect this "self" with every strategy at our disposal. We attack, we withdraw, we divert, we distract, we lie, we steal, we use, we buy, we do all manner of harmful things in an attempt to feel safer, better, and less at risk. We are not wrong for doing so, but we are deluded, and in our delusion, we are capable of bringing great harm and suffering to ourselves and to others.

Our conditioned mind is founded on the fearful assumption that we are separate from everyone and everything else. It is this fearful assumption that sets up the very concept of forgiveness, for only a separate self can be harmed and only a separate self feels the need for forgiveness.

So forgiveness is a necessary practice in our experience of life, for many parts of our psyche truly believe that they are separate, at risk, and vulnerable. For these parts within all of us we compassionately practice forgiveness. But for this practice to be effective it must be rooted in the deeper truth of our identity as part of the Tao. It must spring from our Tao Mind in order to heal our conditioned fears and wounds.

The effects of living in a nightmare are not trivial. The acceptance and compassion of the Tao Mind is not a cavalier dismissal of damage done. It is a willingness to open oneself to the pain, shame, tears, and fears that grow from the beliefs of the conditioned mind, and a willingness to work with the effects of those beliefs in practical and healing ways. At the same time, the Tao Mind does not believe the dreams of separation and fear. Therein lies its power.

We must treat our conditioned, fearful sub-personalities with the same compassionate care that the villagers extended to Maya. We must accept them, forgive them their fears and the acting out that springs from their fears, do what we can to care for them, but, like the villagers, we must not let them be free to wreak their havoc in our lives. We do not need to punish them in order to control them. We can accept the very young, very frightened parts of ourselves but we do not let them handle our bank accounts, drive our cars, dominate our relationships, or make our life decisions for us. We certainly do not let them be in charge of the process of forgiveness.

Questions for Your Tao Mind

- *What nightmares seem the most real to you?*
- *How should you treat yourself when you act in harmful ways?*
- *How should you treat others who act in harmful ways?*
- *What place does punishment play in your experience of forgiveness?*

A Tao Mind Exercise

- *This will be a "three-chair" exercise. Place two straight-back chairs facing your cushion or chair that represents your Tao Mind.*
- *Sit in one of the straight chairs and let your mind remember an event or*

action that stirs a sense of shame or regret in you. See yourself in the midst of this event and feel the sensations in your body, the stories in your mind, and the feelings and emotions that arise.

- *Stand and take three deep, relaxing breaths. Then sit in the Tao Mind seat.*
- *From this perspective observe the chair you just left. Sense both the compassionate acceptance and the willingness to let the pain of the remembered event serve to keep the heart open. Remember—the Tao Mind is not afraid of painful memories or of intense emotions. It is capable of turning both into openhearted compassionate awareness.*
- *Now sit in the other straight chair. This time let your mind remember another person's actions that have been hurtful. Imagine that you are that person. This will require some concentration. We naturally veer aside to judgments and opinions when trying to put ourselves in the place of other people who have caused harm. Suppose the actions stemmed entirely from a nightmare—what are you feeling? Of what are you afraid? What were you trying to do for yourself with this action?*
- *Stand and take three deep, relaxing breaths. Sit down in the Tao Mind seat.*
- *From this perspective observe the chair where the person sat. What does your Tao Mind observe? Remember—the Tao Mind is perfectly capable of taking action to protect you and others from harmful actions when necessary.*

- *Take some time to note your feelings, thoughts, and insights in your journal.*
- *Stand and bow in gratitude to each chair, then to your Tao Mind seat.*

A Tao Mind Meditation

When I dream of falling off a cliff,
I awake with beating heart and panting breath.
My body believes the dream.
In my waking life I believe many dreams:
That I am separate and alone,
That some people can harm my deepest self,
That I can harm their deepest selves,
That no one cares about me,
That I am unlovable and inadequate.
These dreams seem oh, so real.
I would like to wake up.
I am afraid to wake up.
I am willing to wake up.

Ten Thousand Points

A gracious gift cannot be earned.

One evening, just after the final meditation of the day, Anne, the youngest monk at the monastery, was putting out the flame on the beautiful antique lamp that provided a flickering and meditative background in the spacious meditation hall. As she placed the snuffing tool over the flame, she was distracted by the scuttling noise of a squirrel scampering across the terra-cotta tiles of the roof. She turned suddenly and caught the edge of the lamp with the long snuffing tool. The lamp teetered for a moment, then fell onto the edge of the brass bell that sounded the beginning and end of meditation. It shattered, and Anne's heart froze.

Tearfully she swept up the pieces of the lovely lamp and cleaned up the spilled oil. She took the pieces to her teacher and confessed her mistake in great sorrow. The teacher loved the lamp. It was a present from her own teacher and she could not hide her own sadness as she heard the news. Because everyone was aware of the value of the lamp and its special place in the teacher's heart, she knew that Anne would have great difficulty letting go of this mistake. So she spoke sternly to the young monk. "You must find a way to experience forgiveness for this deed. I'll tell you what—each week you come to me with a list of the good acts you have done during the week and I'll give you a certain number of points for such actions. When you reach ten thousand points, you will be able to feel forgiveness."

"Ten thousand points," Anne said. "That's a lot."

"It was a very special lamp," the teacher said in somber tones.

Anne spent the next week doing her work with extra diligence. She diced the potatoes for dinner with special care. She polished the fixtures in the bathrooms until everything shone. She planted the spring seedlings with meticulous care. She meditated with intense concentration. When she met with the teacher at the end of the week, she told of the extraordinary care she had taken with her work and her practice. The teacher smiled and said, "Very, very good. You have shown great care and worked very hard. I am pleased with your diligence." She took out a small notebook, made an entry in it, and said, "That's one point."

One point! Anne was in shock. She staggered back to her room in despair. "It will be ten thousand weeks before I am forgiven. I'll never be able to get over this. I must have caused my teacher such pain." She cried herself to sleep that night.

Several weeks went by and Anne continued to try with all her might to earn her teacher's forgiveness. Each week, despite her efforts, she earned only one point. But a strange thing began to happen. She began to enjoy her mindful and attentive work just because it felt good to work in that manner. One week, as she showed up for her meeting with the teacher, she realized that she had forgotten to keep track of her work. When the teacher asked, "And how have you done this week?" she replied:

"I didn't keep track. I just enjoyed my work."

The teacher's face broke into a broad grin. "That's ten thousand points," she announced.

The essence of the freedom of forgiveness is self-forgiveness. No matter how many forgiving words are spoken by the offended person to the person who committed the offense, the offender will not experience the true Tao of Forgiveness until they bestow it upon themselves from the compassion of their own heart.

The forgiveness one person communicates to another has a certain importance. It sets the stage for a restored relationship. The restitution the offender is able to make for their actions also contributes to the healing of the wounds. Replacing broken lamps, paying for damages, and doing whatever else is possible to mitigate the harm caused can be good and helpful.

But forgiveness itself cannot be earned. Earning forgiveness is an illusion of the conditioned mind, set up to tantalize us into thinking we can somehow "make it right" while at the same time ensuring that "making it right" is an impossible, ten-thousand-point endeavor. Our conditioned mind will always hold on to the memories of the event in such a way as to keep the event alive in its shame and guilt. Even when the offended person tells us sincerely that they forgive us, the freedom of that forgiveness will not be real until we bestow it upon ourselves from the gracious spaciousness of our own Tao Mind.

The title of the old Methodist hymn "Amazing Grace" captures the feeling we have when, after weeks, months, or years of trying to work our way out of the condemnation to which our conditioned mind clings with all its strength, we finally take a breath and step into the generous compassion of our Tao Mind. There is not, nor has there ever been, any condemnation within the Tao Mind. It is a place of amazing grace.

• • • •

Our conditioned mind argues, "I don't want to be without condemnation. Without feeling condemned I will grow careless and do other harmful things. There has to be condemnation."

Yes, we are quite used to the idea that condemnation produces the desired change for the better so we make sure we hold on to it. A certain sub-personality within our ego-structure will attach itself to the condemnation process, listening ceaselessly to a voice that reminds it of the faults and flaws that led to some harmful action. As terrible as this process feels, it gives this sub-personality a twisted sense of security, a self-identity that, though flawed and faulty, has a familiarity about it that seems preferable to the unknown territory of forgiveness.

Until we are willing to give up the security of condemnation, we will avoid taking that step into the freedom of our Tao Mind. Bless our hearts, we are so afraid to give up the familiar patterns of our conditioned mind. We have convinced ourselves that awful things will happen if we are truly free. We do not trust the compassionate wisdom of our Tao Mind to guide us along non-harmful paths.

Let's be gentle with ourselves. We can't bully ourselves into our Tao Mind. Perhaps we can find a small bit of willingness to consider that the process of con-

demnation actually hasn't brought us the growth and goodness it seems to promise. What might it be like to spend five minutes without condemnation? What
would we do if we followed, not the conflicting voices and counter-voices of our
conditioning, but our natural instinct to be kind, mindful, and aware?

Questions for Your Tao Mind

- *What is the role of restitution in the forgiveness process?*
- *Who benefits from restitution?*
- *What if restitution is not possible?*

A Tao Mind Exercise

- *Arrange two chairs facing each other—one to represent a sub-personality
within you who is feeling, hearing, and experiencing persistent voices of
condemnation, the other chair representing your Tao Mind.*
- *Sit with your journal in the "Chair of Condemnation." Write down
everything you are being told about yourself from this position.*

- *Stand and stretch. Take ten full relaxed breaths and sit in the Tao Mind chair.*
- *Let your posture be open and without tension. Look at each thing you wrote from the perspective of the Chair of Condemnation. Mindfully and carefully, cross each of these out. Put a big bold "X" through each letter of each sentence.*
- *Sit with your journal and start a new page. Title the page "Condemnations." Leave the page completely blank. Notice what your conditioning wants to tell you about the blank page. Notice feelings and sensations. How might it feel to live a life in which there was no condemnation whatsoever?*
- *Stand, stretch, and breathe. Go about your daily life by doing the very next thing that comes to mind.*

A Tao Mind Meditation

Feeling flawed and wrong,
I know who I am.
Earning my worth,
I know what to do.

Without condemnation,
I am frightened.
I don't know who I am
or what to do.
Waiting and breathing in freedom,
I know only the next simple step.
It is enough.

A Final Word of
Blessing and Encouragement

Forgiveness is so simple and so easy, yet so complex and so difficult. Like the Tao, it can't be told in words but it can be experienced in life. I hope my combination of story and commentary has been helpful in pointing to the blessings and freedom of forgiveness. It may be helpful to review some of the images and themes that I have used in my attempt to point to that which cannot be told in words.

- *Feeling the lack of forgiveness is like standing outside the gate leading into a beautiful meadow. Going through the gate, we realize that forgiveness has always been, and always will be, a natural part of our life. Only our narrow perspective keeps us from it.*

- *Practicing forgiveness leads us to face basic questions of identity. Who are we? What parts of us hold on? What parts of us are willing to let go? Is there a deeper part, a more mysterious part to whom we can turn?*

- *Forgiveness allows us to use the harm we do to reveal and affirm the tenderness that is naturally ours.*

- *Anger, though a natural emotion, keeps opinions and beliefs locked in place within conditioned mind and does not allow room to move into Tao Mind forgiveness. We can feel intense passion, commitment, and energy without holding on to anger.*

- *We are all doing the best we know how to do. Forgiveness is the process by which harm transforms into benefit as long as we don't hold on to rigid ideas of which is which.*

- *The very blessing of our mind that allows us to plan, anticipate, and imagine also sets us up for disappointment. Our response to disappointment in ourselves and in others will either constrict our lives or open them to forgiveness and freedom.*

- *Words like "I'm sorry" and "I forgive you" can be tricky. Words can carry great depths of emotion and sincerity, but they remain pointers to forgiveness and not the thing itself.*

- *There is a difference between truly wanting the freedom of forgiveness and* just wanting to "feel better." Actually stepping into freedom can be difficult and frightening and we often settle for clinging to our guilt or resentment.

• Certain acts are considered so "bad" that forgiveness seems impossible. Yet in Tao Mind, nothing can ever put a person outside of acceptance. In these situations the conditioned mind can never bring us the relief we seek. We must look elsewhere.

• Our sense of identity can get wrapped up in being either "right" or "wrong." Taking the actions of others as personal affronts is not helpful even though it seems so true. If we are "taking it personally," we are keeping a sense of ego-identity in place that may not be serving us.

• The habitual act of blaming—either ourselves or others—keeps us stuck in a futile attempt to control life. If we can lay the blame at someone's feet, we can hang on to the illusion that, if we just get everyone to behave, nothing bad will happen. Finding forgiveness requires a relinquishment of the blame habit.

• We become so used to carrying the burdens created by a lack of forgiveness that we are strangely reluctant to lay them down, even when someone points out that there is no need to carry them. It is helpful to realize that forgiveness of the Tao Mind waits patiently for as long as it takes for us to be willing to stop.

- *Memories, though precious and necessary, can be a hindrance to finding the freedom of forgiveness. They are selective and usually interpreted through the filters of our conditioned mind. Keeping the "remembering" process spacious and gentle rather than snarled and tight allows access to the Tao Mind.*
- *Like the sound of ocean surf, the freedom of forgiveness is an ever-present background to our life. The noise and chatter of our conditioned thoughts attempts to keep us stuck in blame, but relief can be as simple as listening to our breath go in and out.*
- *Our conditioned mind trains us to see other people through a set of assumptions that are quite limited. We can remain stuck in resentment because we have assumed certain things about the motivations, actions, and words of other people. The Tao Mind contains no assumptions and is able to present us with a clear perspective of our own actions and the actions of others.*
- *If we attempt to have only comfortable and acceptable experiences in our life, we cut ourselves off from Life Itself. Confident in our Tao Mind's ability to accept and forgive, we are able to wade into any situation with a sense of adventure and adequacy.*
- *When the conditioned mind creates the categories of "friend" and "enemy," it leads us into a narrow experience of other people. Forgiveness becomes*

*reserved for certain categories and we may end up isolated and resentful—
our own worst "enemy."*

- *Our Tao Mind is never afraid of "being wrong." Mistakes are seen as
  marvelous opportunities for growth. Forgiveness is the essential quality that
  transforms "wrong" and "mistake" into "wonderful opportunity."*

- *Life contains dangerous, even fatal, situations. War, natural disasters,
  accidents, illness that strikes out of the blue, and many other realities of life
  present us with the opportunity to actually "forgive Life"—to accept and find
  ourselves capable of everything life presents to us.*

- *We all have attachment to certain external and internal "rules." Any
  behavior that falls outside our own personal "rule book" frightens us and
  lessens the sense of control and safety we experience. Forgiveness asks us to
  look at the way we react to "rule-breaking" in ourselves and in others. Are
  rules whips for punishment or guideposts for growth?*

- *Our actions have sometimes truly harmed others and we have sometimes
  been truly harmed by theirs. Understanding that every person is capable of
  healing and being completely adequate for whatever life brings them helps us
  let go and move on when our conditioned mind tries to convince us that we
  must hold on and neither forgive nor forget.*

- *Punishment seldom facilitates the forgiveness process. Protecting oneself and one's community is a natural and legitimate action. But letting fear shift self-protection into punishing others inhibits forgiveness and actually lessens personal safety.*

- *By the very nature of the Tao Mind, forgiveness cannot be earned. It is always freely given. But the Tao Mind uses a creative interplay of restitution and generous grace in order to facilitate our ability to accept and make forgiveness a reality in our experience.*

Bless you for your willingness to read the words that I have offered in this book. As I have repeated throughout the book, it is your willingness that brings you into the freedom of forgiveness.

May you have the willingness:

- *to trust that forgiveness in all of its spacious graciousness is already the truth of your life and of all other lives.*
- *to trust that your own true nature is fundamentally compassionate, kind, and whole.*
- *to allow yourself to experience those moments in which all the burdens, shames, and resentments to which we all so readily cling disappear into the infinite nature of your Tao Mind.*

- *to be patient with yourself when your conditioned mind quickly closes off those moments and returns you to the familiar cacophony of the voices of judgment, condemnation, and fear.*
- *to be open to your own Tao Mind, in which you may discover that "there is no self and other," and through which all of your wounds and the wounds of all beings will be healed.*

Our struggles to forgive and be forgiven are universal. Our longing for freedom is shared by all beings. If writing to me to express your own experience would be helpful for you, you are most welcome to do so. I can be reached through the website of our center, The Still Point. Any communication to me through that site is completely confidential and will be read only by me—www.thestillpoint.com.

May any benefit that arises from this book be for the forgiveness and freedom of all beings everywhere. May any harm that arises from this book be accepted, forgiven, and turned again by Tao Mind into tenderness and openhearted living.

Acknowledgments

My agent, Barbara Moulton, has been my friend for years. She encouraged and placed my first book and has since patiently watched, supported, accepted, and most of all, forgiven me. This book exists because of her.

Joel Fotinos at Tarcher had the idea for this book and trusted me to bring it to life. It is not something I would have attempted left to my own devices. This book exists because of him.

Thirty-two people from around the world joined me for a six-month e-mail discussion of "Forgiveness." They were willing to look at their own processes of holding on and of letting go. Their honesty, courage, and acceptance of one another has been a profound example to me of the reality of the Tao Mind. This book exists because of them.

Lao-tzu left the world eighty-one short chapters, only five thousand words, that express the Mystery of the Tao. Bless him. I'm not sure I would be alive today if not for him. This book exists because he first wrote the *Tao Te Ching.*

My spouse, Nancy, lives the forgiveness I have tried to express. She sees all of my sub-personalities, loves them all, forgives them all, and has shown me my own intrinsic nature. This book exists because of her.

Thank you all.